From the Inside Out:

Therapists' Confessions of Courage, Strength, and Hope

Co-authored and Compiled by

Jacqueline Rech, MS LPC

From the Inside Out: Therapists' Confessions of Courage, Strength, and Hope

© 2019 Jacqueline Rech, MS LPC

www.TherapistsConfessions.com

All rights reserved. Printed in the United States of America and Canada. No part of this book may be used or reproduced in any manner whatsoever without written permission from the author, except in the case of brief quotations within critical articles or reviews.

Although the authors and publisher have made every effort to ensure that the information in this book was correct at press time, the authors and publisher do not assume and hereby disclaim any liability to any party due to these words coming from the authors' own opinion based on their experiences.

Every word in this book is based on the authors' experience of their personal development journey and the outcomes with clients that they may have witnessed. Although we have made every reasonable attempt to achieve complete accuracy in the content of this book, we assume no responsibility for errors or omissions in the information in this book.

You should only use this information as you see fit at your own risk. Your life and circumstances may not be suited to these examples with what we share within these pages.

Editing, cover design, and formatting by www.letsgetbooked.com

Print ISBN: 978-0-578-58189-7

For those who suffer in silence

This book is for you

We hope our stories help guide you out of darkness,

Leaving your hearts and minds renewed

For Your Attention:

This book contains material that may evoke strong emotions.

There is some use of adult language and discussion of the following:

Childhood Sexual Trauma

Intimate Partner Violence

Divorce

Foster Care

Depression and Anxiety

Faith and Spirituality

Codependency

Food Insecurity

Suicidal Ideation and Attempts

Eating Disorders

Self-Harming Behaviors

Alcoholism and Addiction

Parent with Addiction

Childhood Emotional Neglect

Personal Mental Illness

Immigration

Incarceration

Bullying

Death of a Child / Parent / Spouse

Homicide

Suicide

Postpartum Depression and Anxiety

You will find a resource list at the back of this book starting on page 249 organized by each author's chapter and content area if you find that you are struggling.

Remember to take steps to care for yourself before, during, and after reading this book. Please reach out to someone if you need.

TABLE OF CONTENTS

FOREWORD   1
INTRODUCTION   4
PART ONE   11
    1. Lost and Found   13
    2. Journeys Converging   26
    3. Permission to be a Human   39
    4. Broken Together   53
    5. Breaking Stigma   64
    6. My Tapestry   74
    7. Between Two Worlds   84
    8. Perfectly Imperfect   93
    9. Bitter or Better   104
    10. Blessed by the Broken Road   113
    11. Grieving with Grit, Grace, and Gratitude   127
PART TWO   137
    1. The Potter's Wheel   139
    2. Kintsugi   148
    3. Healing is a Verb   158
    4. It Takes a Village   173
    5. A Darkness Within   185
    6. The Blind Side   194

7.	Moving Forward with Purpose	204
8.	Eyes on the Prize	214
9.	Sharing is Caring	223
10.	On Being a Therapist	233

ACKNOWLEDGEMENTS	242
REFERENCES	246
RESOURCE LIST	249

FOREWORD

Little did I realize on the day I responded to a post in a Facebook professional peer group that I would be embarking on a journey that would encompass a year to complete. Nor could I anticipate the far-reaching and lasting impact that decision would make on my life's path. The timing of my meeting Jackie was karma, as they say. It happened at just the right time. I have always thought of writing a book for as long as I can remember, but I always brushed it aside as I believed that it was beyond my abilities and resources. Once Jackie and I began exploring what this process would entail, and this book began to solidify, the connection and energy between us grew and the book took on a life of its own. I began to see that putting a book together and actually having it out there for you to read was going to happen! It was both exhilarating and empowering! I will be forever grateful for the opportunity to be a part of that process, and to share my story with you.

One of my passions is for the performing arts. Performing live theater gives me a similar feeling of connection and energy, and for me, there is nothing like it. I can literally feel when my fellow actors 'get' my intention through my voice and my actions, and we play off each other. The audience's reaction shows if they, too, are engrossed and engaged with the story playing out on stage. And for me, that give and take adds to the 'high' of the experience. There is nothing like it.

As you'll read later in my story, I drifted away from performing after meeting my first husband, and I lost my connection with a collective force that fueled my passion and creativity. I discovered that as mine and Jackie's roles in the creative process of bringing this book to fruition grew and evolved, my sense of passion and purpose returned. I felt that old "fire in the belly" as they say! My confidence soared, and I became excited as I imagined an audience picking up this book and it forever touching their lives.

The stories these therapists share and the chapters that follow are a call to you, dear reader, to begin a search of your own. Let it be an amazing journey that includes the fuel that nourishes your soul, fosters your beliefs, and defines your individual and special path towards well-being. I hope you never lose sight of the need and desire to reconnect all the parts and passions that make you you and allowing them to reinvigorate your own healing process.

We live in a society that promotes connection through the use of technology over face-to-face communication, and individuality and independence over community. This occurrence has both helped and hindered the therapeutic process by promoting a "go it alone" attitude that hinders motivation to seek out professional help. It is becoming easier to avoid face-to-face connection with the outside world and as a consequence, we're losing our connection as human beings. Thus, the thought of going to a perfect stranger and "baring one's soul" has become even more foreign. Yet, you have more control over personal interactions than you realize dear reader! It's not just one-sided.

When it comes to the therapeutic process, I'm a little more relaxed than most therapists, perhaps, when it comes to self-disclosure. I don't mean that I bare my soul in session. One of the best insights I received from my various teachers and mentors was that there are themes to life's experiences. The human condition is the 'human' condition. By sharing a relatable experience in session, I normalize the experiences and emotions that come with it, and I offer a different perspective on working through them. You will read about many relatable experiences in the following pages. It is my hope that this book can help provide a safe space to explore your thoughts and emotions and normalize them. We offer a different perspective on working through some very difficult life situations and events. Okay, I digress. Now, take a deep breath, because it's time for our journey together to begin as we share our experiences. Let us come alongside you while you reflect on your own human condition and contemplate steps towards building resilience, insight, and fortitude for the journey ahead.

Ellen

INTRODUCTION

So here I am writing a book; a book I never thought would become a reality. You are literally holding a dream nine years in the making in your hands. I am sitting in my makeshift office area in the basement as the sealant for the desk I built for upstairs dries. Both of my children are sleeping, and my husband is upstairs washing dishes. If I don't take time to sit down now to start writing this book, then it won't get started (hello mom brain! It's a real thing, I swear!) I'm just a mom ... well, not *just* a mom. Once upon a time, I was a clinical therapist and I loved being active in my career field. Sure, I always said if I could do it all over again, I'd be a finish carpenter, motivational speaker, event planner, personal assistant, furniture designer ... the list goes on. So why a therapist? That, my friends, is a good question. I decided to become a therapist initially because it seemed 'easier' before I ever sat down for a college course. I spent my life doing everything I could to understand the world around me through my interactions with the people in it. I observed them, and constantly made mental notes to myself on how to behave based on their examples ... well, how to react is probably more accurate. But since that time, I've met so many people who were hurting and in need of quality therapy from a professional who respected them and could help them believe in and reach their full potential. I wanted to become the kind of therapist that could best serve the people around me. So, I chose an educational path honoring that desire, and so began my journey towards becoming the therapist I am today.

Most of my life has been lived from one traumatic situation and chaotic disaster to the next. It wasn't until I became older that I realized my childhood was not the most "normal" of childhoods. It was then that I wondered what made me different. How did I survive my experiences relatively unscathed, rather than be lost in the constant darkness that surrounded me? When I spoke with other people in my field, I discovered that they had similar stories and backgrounds. So, I thought, *Is this just in my field? Are therapists a special breed of people?* The obvious answer to that is *no*. No, therapists aren't some superhuman species set aside to 'fix' the world. By the way, I'd like to add that therapists aren't in the business of 'fixing' anything. They come alongside you to facilitate awareness, challenge you to shift your perspective, and support you in ways that do not enable you to continue in self-destructive or abusive behaviors. But I digress. What was I writing? ... (Pausing for a mom brain moment) ... Ahh, right. Superhuman therapists. We aren't superhuman. In fact, so many of us have lived so many different lives, and have a plethora of life experiences from which we can pull from in order to better empathize with and assist you in navigating the choppy waters of your current life situation, or past trauma.

But guess what? We weren't *really* able to tell you any of those experiences.

Until now.

Professional distance and ethics are meant to help protect each of us during the therapeutic process. They allow us to meet you where you are in your stuff without taking that stuff home with us. If we did not care for ourselves in this way, we would surely burn out faster than a sparkler on the Fourth of July. It would be as if you went into a house fire without protective gear on. You might avoid the actual flames, but you'd surely succumb to smoke inhalation or the heat (I'm still wrecked over that episode of *This is Us*).

Another reason you've never heard our stories is because you aren't our therapist. We are yours. We are in our position to care *for you*. And that takes skill and forethought. It takes artistry that we have developed over time. It is a dance in which you lead, and we follow. We do not focus on us in session because we are in session to focus on you. And if we want to do our best job possible, we need to leave our own mess behind. The moment we step into our offices, the traffic jam, arguments we had with our own spouses, the worries about our ailing parents … all of it has to be left outside the door so we can fully enter into and provide a nurturing and healthy space for you. It is our duty as therapists to process all our own stuff with our own therapist so that we do not take it out on you. A surgeon does not ask her patient to begin cutting out her own cancer while she's in the middle of cutting out theirs. Nor does she arrive at surgery unlearned, unprepared, and unfamiliar with the tools laid out before her. She knows exactly which tools are used for which procedure. She is in control of her tools and uses them with skill and precision. Any ailments she has are cared for by her own physician, and if she is too tired or too ill to work, she doesn't. She spends time to care for herself and then returns to take care of her patients. If she does not take care of herself, then she is risking the lives of her patients. And so are we, as therapists, if we do not care for ourselves and allow transference or countertransference to interfere with the ultra-important work of coming alongside to support and challenge you.

There is also a disclosure barrier. Remember, we're here for *you*. Not for us. We will not waste precious time unraveling or unpacking our own stuff for you to look at, think about, and inspect. We do not want you leaving our presence overwhelmed or otherwise focused on us. The journey you're on is your own, and we are not going to place our own stumbling blocks in your way. Sure, we may share some tidbits as a means of relating to you, but you'll never hear an unabridged, and unedited telling of our life stories.

That's why I wanted to write this book. Many times, while in session over the years I wanted to stand up and shout, "I have been where you are! I was divorced, too! I know loneliness and abandonment, too!" But I couldn't, lest I interrupt my client's own process, or thoughts, to insert my own. You should also know that I love Jesus. He is the milk to my cookie, peanut butter to my jelly; he is my *jam*. And even though I am nowhere even close to being anything that would resemble perfect or good, my life experiences are seen through the lens of my faith. So, you should know that now before we continue. It's okay if Jesus isn't your jam. We're all diffcrent, and that's what makes this world a beautiful place. But I always felt that God allowed me to experience so many different types of situations for a purpose. I searched for life's meaning—all the bits of it. I always felt that my life experiences were like an appetizer tray: I lived them long enough to really let the taste sink in and be felt with all of my senses and carved into my heart and mind, but not long enough that my life seemed beyond healing and recovery. I always thought that my cumulative life experiences are what really helped me relate to my clients in real and meaningful ways. Except, I could never really share those experiences. So, I thought I'd write a book about them, but a book about my life, though fascinating as it may be (can you hear the sarcasm in that statement?) would be boring and not very effective if it stood alone. I wanted to share this platform with others.

A strand of three is not easily broken. But what about a strand of five? Or, in our case, eleven? There is strength and power in numbers. I wanted you to hear the stories of many of us. Stories that left us so broken that we couldn't get up without help. Stories that left us so lost in darkness that we couldn't find our way back out alone. These are stories from therapists … not about their caseloads, or unique clients. These stories are from their own personal lives ... the lives lived hidden behind the curtain for no one but their own therapists to see and hear. Therapy is a key component of these stories as well, because without the very hard work of processing through their own stuff they could not stand autonomous from their pasts in a way that would allow them to live healthy, giving, and productive lives. It was important to me for each therapist to share their story from a place of healthy reflection. Each story is shared with power, and a desire to help change your life.

This book will be split into two parts. In part one, you will read our own stories and of the courage, strength, and hope it took for us to reach up and out of our circumstances so that we could invest our passion and energy into others. It is our hope that the story itself is what will inspire hope that whatever you're facing can be overcome, healed from, and mended. In part two, you will begin to explore ways to think about your own lived experiences. There will be questions for you to reflect on or journal about. I hope the second half of the book will help you decide where you are in your readiness to embark on your own healing journey.

Our hope is that you're able to connect with the humanity shared in the pages of this book among a group of people society views as life mechanics. We do not fix things. Or people. We do not work from a place that assumes you are broken. I want you to understand that we all begin life born into different circumstances, are then bombarded with a myriad of life experiences, and respond to these challenges in different ways. We stand together and apart. Side by side. We want to share our stories of courage, strength, and hope so that you know you are not alone. Chances are the therapist you know has experience in an area you are quite familiar with, and you both can connect with that shared pain of loss, heartache, abandonment, or abuse. Our stories reveal the journey we took that turned tragedy into trajectory, abuse into abundance, loss into laughter, and harm into hope. So, sit back, and relax as us therapists take a turn at this storytelling thing.

Jackie

Co-authored and Compiled by Jacqueline Rech

PART ONE

"Tell the story of the mountains you climbed. Your words could become a page in someone else's survival guide."

– MORGAN HARPER NICHOLS [1]

Co-authored and Compiled by Jacqueline Rech

CHAPTER ONE:

Lost and Found

Jacqueline Rech, MS LPC

If you were to meet me years ago, you'd see a smiling face and happy demeanor because I learned to adapt to the cultural expectations of how I should present myself. Inside, you would have seen an insecure, lonely, and abandoned girl consumed by anger, pain, disappointment, resentment, and unforgiveness. You would see all the criticisms, and judgements I reserved for myself and others who hurt me. Basically, you'd find my heart as a dark and desolate place filled with pain. I lost all hope that I would find love, or true friendship, or the ability to walk in a room and feel that I deserved to be there. I felt like I was always roaming, always searching but after thirty moves in just as many years, I still hadn't found what I was looking for.

My life began unexpectedly when my mother, according to family, made an at home attempt to end her pregnancy. This attempt eventually led to my very premature birth. It wouldn't be until some thirty years later that I would learn the man she left me with, and who raised me—my father, and the man she married—wasn't actually my biological father. But he was the most convenient choice to raise the child she seemed to not want or need. My brother was born ten months later, and it wasn't long afterward that she left our family to join the military. One of my earliest memories was of her leaving out the door, promising me that she'd come back after working with something called 'computers'. She never came back for us. Her sudden departure left gaping wounds in mine and my brother's tiny hearts, but a seemingly bigger hole in our father's.

We moved around a lot, as my father struggled with being a newly single father to two very young children while in his early to mid-twenties. Throughout this period of time, my brother and I knew that our dad loved us. He might not have made the best decisions, but he tried his best. He had things he needed to work through, and over the years I think he'd say he grew to be the man, husband, and father he wished he could have been during this particular season. Today we have a caring and supportive relationship, but back then he was young and struggling. When he wasn't up all night partying or working multiple jobs, he was sleeping during the day. These parties exposed us to some unsafe people. Another of my earliest memories was waking up to a trauma at the age of four.

[**Trigger warning** ... I can still feel the wetness on my face falling down on me as I looked up to make sense of what was happening. Whatever else had occurred must have been so traumatizing that my memory includes seeing myself from behind, as I dissociated from the trauma. I have an amazing visual memory. I can recall the pattern in the sofa I woke up on, yet no matter how often I've replayed my time in that house, there is still a room there that I cannot account for or 'see', and that worries me sometimes.]

These memories would surface a few years later, and then again after high school. I would come to understand them as repressed memories, only surfacing when my body was completely drained of the mental, emotional, and physical energy and effort it must have taken to keep them down. This usually happened during big life changes, like entering foster care, or college, for example. It was also during this difficult fourth year of life that we struggled with food insecurity, and I felt like a mother to my then three-year-old brother. While our father slept, I taught myself how to use the microwave, and ensure my brother was bathed and fed. We were in survival mode, enduring other trauma throughout this time. We were so young, unable to trust other children or adults or any sense of stability they may have tried to offer us.

Our mother was gone, and I watched her leave with my own eyes. Naturally, this meant that I would continue to search for her for several years. Anytime I was in the back of a car, I would look out to the horizon for as far as I could see, and imagine that my mother was *just on the other side*. I decided the reason I couldn't see her was because of the limits of my own eyes. I blamed my eyesight for her absence, instead of her own choice to remain hidden from us. She did not want to be found. I know this because as an adult I looked for her.

Instability and lack of trust followed me and my relationships from this point on. By the time I was eight, I had been shuffled around between three states, multiple extended family homes, and moved ten times. My eleventh destination was a foster home. I did not understand the adult world in which this choice was made. It felt like one day I was home, and the next day I watched my father leave us in a stranger's house. Again, I was watching the back of another parent leave us. Our foster mother tried to provide some structure and stability in the year we spent with her, but she spent hours in her room studying for exams. We were often left alone with her son, who was two years older than me, her elderly aunt, or her mother. Our foster brother bullied my brother and I, and his grandmother spent her time ignoring us or slinging racial slurs at me, as I looked more Asian than my brother. When my foster brother called me a beggar in front of my friend and her parents, I vowed to never ask anyone for anything ever again. We would return to our father at the end of the school year when he and my stepmother married.

Our stepmother was very young, and just graduated from college. She had a lot to learn about being a mother. She did not realize we had experienced trauma. The many parenting books she read during her first years with us did not prepare her for how to nurture and care for children like us. That wasn't a topic they covered. My stepmother did her best, but even so, I felt a disconnect between us. My view of our relationship shifted when I read in her journal her desire to have a "child of her own." She later provided closure over this incident by explaining her words stemmed from feeling left out of the family unit she married into. She desired to have someone she could better relate with, and who could share something of hers. At the time, though, I was crushed, and any hope I had for a close-knit mother/daughter relationship was destroyed. She provided our basic needs, but her very reserved nature did not lend itself to providing the type of love, affection, and acceptance we were searching for. My continued search led me down some dark places. I would make some poor decisions from a heart, mind, and body that had been through so much.

Throughout school, I had decided that I was going to be the exact opposite of the mother who I felt abandoned us. I spent most of my time focused on my studies, and made it to college. It was during this transition that my repressed memories resurfaced. I didn't know how else to deal with them than to distract myself with alcohol, and parties on campus. This ruined my academic career and undid all the hard work I invested to this point. I eventually realized the stupidity of my ways, but instead of seeking out therapy, I put all my time and energy into a relationship with a boy I had just met. He was charming, handsome, funny, and affectionate. In him, I thought I had finally found someone who would care for me, protect me, love me, and connect with me in a way I had never experienced before. Instead, nearly nine years with him were marked with deceit, chaos, trauma, and repeated infidelity. I became hypervigilant, following him places he probably should not have been. By this time, I was hooked on whatever time and affection he decided to give me. I felt I could not leave, despite the repeated betrayals and chaos. In time, he chose to get the support he needed, and we were married. We continued to struggle in other ways, and eventually, infidelity ended our short two-and-a-half-year marriage, just as I was finishing up my bachelor's degree.

I still had yet to seek therapy, even though I *really* needed it. They say the first cut is the deepest, and man, that divorce cut deep! I lost myself and went on a spree of bad decision making that can still make me feel shame and embarrassment if I think about it too much. So, when I met my second husband, he seemed to be a breath of fresh air. What follows is my opinion of him and our relationship, and events in this book are how I remembered them. I did not realize that I was the perfect wounded prey for his snare. By the time I met him, my self-esteem had been destroyed. The only thing I had to hold onto was my performance-based identity. Grades felt safe as they were objective and measurable. I entered grad school while dating him. And he presented himself as the most perfect example of a man he could be. We attended church and bible study together. But hidden underneath the facade seemed to me to be a darkened and selfish heart thriving on the ability to make others see and believe in whatever version of himself he wanted them to. I felt that it filled him with a sense of power, and control. In hindsight, I feel he might have had difficulty hiding some less-than-ideal parts of his personality. It makes sense to me, then, why he moved so quickly to secure my commitment to him. We were engaged and married within our first year of dating. The week of our wedding I started to experience a side to his personality—as if a different person altogether. I shrugged these mood swings off as 'cold feet'. However, all pretenses were dropped once the reception was over. On our way home from our honeymoon, he had become so angry that he refused to speak to me. I didn't know what triggered this response, but when we arrived back to his place, he demanded that I leave. I hadn't even moved in yet, and had nowhere to go. The short ten weeks I stayed under his roof were filled with verbal and emotional chaos. I felt like I was walking on eggshells. I couldn't believe the mess I had gotten myself into. How could I have been so stupid and naive? I felt deceived, and crushed.

Four weeks into our marriage, I decided enough was enough and I entered marriage counseling. Alone. By this point he had already stopped wearing his wedding ring and tossed it in a junk drawer, outright refusing to attend counseling sessions with me.

He would call me at work, and the end result would leave me in tears. I would come to learn the term for this kind of behavior as gas-lighting. I continued to attend counseling sessions alone over the next six weeks and the counselor would go over some red flags within my "marriage". I held on because I didn't want the stigma of being so young and twice divorced. I couldn't believe the person who proposed to me in Times Square on New Year's Eve as the ball dropped was the same person I married.

That person seemed to vanish. I realized I really didn't know the person I married at all. I was also trying to finish my first year of grad school while working full time as a counselor. I was barely holding myself together, and would arrive to class tearful after my most recent contact. Although I had nowhere else to go, I made a promise to myself that if things escalated, I would leave.

I needed to make that decision sooner than I was expecting. I mean, all the red flags were pointing to this eventuality. The last time I was scheduled for marriage counseling, my ex decided the night before he was finally going to attend. However, by the next morning, he changed his mind, angrily dismissing me. Again, I felt completely crushed. That was the straw that broke the camel's back. After weeks of chaos, I mentally and emotionally checked out of my marriage right then and there for this, and so many other things I am unable to retell here. I tried to find a friend to call, and unfortunately, I did—an ex-boyfriend. The next day I returned home intent on ending my marriage, and admitting my infidelity. But before I could get any of that out of my mouth a situation happened (I would later share honestly about it all in a phone conversation). Chaos erupted. And then a moment of clarity interrupted the scene, and all I could say was, "Thank you." At that, I was released from the chaos as I stumbled to regain my footing. He ran away from me and into our bedroom, locked himself in the room, and yelled back at me through the door. What he said to me from behind that closed door made me feel that he blamed me for what had just happened. I thanked him in the midst of it all because it was the permission I needed to give myself a reason to escape. I called my brother who was there in minutes to take me back to his apartment where I laid awake the rest of the night replaying what would be the end of my second marriage. I didn't have anywhere to go. My parents didn't have room for me. Thankfully, a coworker invited me to stay in her stepdaughter's bedroom, and 'mothered' me as I tried to make sense of the last nine years of my life.

After three months in temporary housing, I found off-campus housing with a friend of mine from grad-school. I had been sleeping on a blowup mattress for two months in this new place before I finally had enough money to buy myself an honest to goodness bed. I finally realized I was safe as I laid across the first bed *I* owned in my entire adulthood. I exhaled and then sobbed. For an entire hour. All the pain and chaos of the last nearly ten years came spilling out and washed over me. When there were no more tears. I realized I needed help. I had just started my second year of grad school, and so I called our university's counseling center and got myself an appointment. I would begin processing *all* my trauma. But after a year, I stopped going. Though I had made so much progress, I still had much more work to do.

Within a year, I met my current husband. He wasn't just fresh air. He was like breathing air on a completely different planet. When we met, I was happily living as a single woman focused on my schoolwork, strengthening my relationship with God, and continuing to process my trauma in therapy. From the beginning, my husband showed me who he was, without pretense, or judgement. He was completely open to me, and I was open to him. He was and still is an amazing man of constant faith, and integrity. He fully accepted all of me, and my entire past, with open arms. This was the kind of relationship I had been searching for. By the time we were married, I had been healed by my faith, and supported that healing through therapy.

I completed grad school and started working in substance abuse treatment. And one year around Mother's Day I had a complete breakdown. I was sobbing in the Target parking lot because I had to buy Mother's Day cards, and their words never described my complicated relationships with mother figures well enough. That same day I made an appointment to see a faith-based therapist. I had given myself time to process my past traumas, but now it was time to process the abandonment I felt, my complicated relationships with mother figures—past and present—and continue on my healing journey. A year into therapy I was feeling great and ready to stop. But I became pregnant, experienced a traumatic miscarriage, then became pregnant again. I was still processing the miscarriage, and found that I had a ton of misgivings about being a mom. What if I couldn't connect with my children? What if I abandoned my children just like my mother did? I spent my entire second pregnancy processing my own anxieties surrounding becoming a mother, and fearing another miscarriage.

When my son was born, I was hit hard with postpartum anxiety. My history of trauma was a big risk factor. And I was okay, until one night I was awake and there was a loud bang in our house. My husband slept right through it, and I had to wake him up to investigate. This set off a trigger in me. I felt like the only one that could protect this baby if something happened. My postpartum anxiety told me I couldn't rely on my husband because clearly, he would just sleep through the threat. That next night began months of severe sleep deprivation. After experiencing two home break-ins in the last decade, I'd stay up all night hypervigilant, straining my ears for any sounds of a third. I'd stare underneath my door at what little light there was for shadows of feet. I imagined every conceivable type of danger, and peril that could befall my new little family, and planned our escape and survival each night for every single scenario. It would be two months before I realized I needed help. In that time, my hypervigilance, and lack of sleep from the postpartum anxiety triggered my PTSD. Then it opened up *all* of my past traumas all over again. I sought out EMDR (eye movement desensitization and reprocessing) therapy, which helped my brain and body to reprocess any traumatic or anxiety-inducing thoughts and feelings so that they didn't trigger a fight or flight response. After eight sessions, I was able to end my treatment, and eventually tapered my other therapy sessions. I was caring for myself, sleeping again, and employing all the tools I learned in EMDR. I no longer feared that I would abandon my children, and eventually forgave my mother, and everyone else that had ever done me harm.

I gave birth to my second child in 2018, and was prepared for the postpartum anxiety. I had my toolkit in place, but was blindsided by postpartum depression. The best I could do was nurse my daughter and feed my son. That was it. I wasn't sleeping again and felt alone in my support community. Again, I found that I needed therapy, and sought it online. I fit in sessions during my children's naptime. I added exercise, proper nutrition, and began using my EMDR tools again. I was still struggling when I began the process for this book last August, when my daughter was only five months old. Thankfully, my postpartum depression fully lifted mid-December and I was able to return to my previous levels of functioning before writing began on this chapter and the rest of this book.

I cannot tell you how important therapy was throughout my healing journey. It was also important that I recognized the signs and symptoms of my declining emotional and physical functioning, so that I could receive the help I needed each time. Processing my past trauma and relationships was vital so that I could be the loving wife and mother my healthy, Christ-centered marriage and children deserved. Each of my therapists walked alongside me. They showed compassion, concern, and care. They allowed me time to sit back and reflect, but also challenged me to face faulty thinking or other behaviors. I am thankful for the way they worked with me, supported me, and nurtured my healing.

You may be sitting there unsure of how you feel about therapy, or faith, or a number of other things in life. But I want you to know it's okay to be unsure. No-one has all the answers. We're all just doing the best we can with the time we have. But it is my heart's desire that you would take some time to reflect on your life and experiences, and if you think you might be willing to share those thoughts with another person, then I would call someone, right now. Really. Right now. Share with them your desire to reach a place of peace, and healing. I promise you, you won't regret it.

Jacqueline Rech, MS LPC

Jacqueline Rech is a work-at-home mother and licensed professional counselor with a Master of Science degree in Clinical Mental Health Counseling, and a Bachelor's of Arts degree in Psychology from California University of Pennsylvania. She most recently worked for a faith-based private practice, and has treated individuals, couples and families. Jacqueline is passionate about walking alongside others as they embark on their healing journeys; more specifically those who struggle with substance abuse, anxiety, depression, and trauma-related issues. When she isn't raising her two very young children, she enjoys freelance writing, photography, snowboarding, spending time with friends and family, and leisurely strolls with an ice cream in hand.

CHAPTER TWO:

Journeys Converging

Ellen Ulmer, LPC, NCC, NAADC

When Jackie reached out with an opportunity to write my story, I jumped at the opportunity without hesitation. Writing about what brought me to this point in my life is like putting a period to a sentence. Not that this is the final stop in my journey; just that seeing my words brings the opportunity for me to find even more clarity and reflect on the people, places, and things that have held me back or moved me forward. You, dear reader, will be privy to some of my innermost thoughts and feelings. You'll find that we all share the basic ability for resilience, we just don't always see how to tap into it. My story is about disappointments, tremendous loss, and never feeling good enough, yet never giving up and always pushing through, finding the small victories in the life challenges that converge into life changers.

Where to begin? Okay, let's start with who I am and why should anything I have to say matter? I'm the youngest of five daughters. I'm a lot younger than my four older sisters as they are seven, eight, thirteen and fourteen years older than I am. By the age of ten, my sisters had gone off to college or were on their own. I was then, more or less, an only child. We have always been a close family. Lots of trips and family gatherings. I was very active in Girl Scouts, dance, gymnastics, theater (which became my passion). My parents were very supportive and encouraged my involvement in all these activities. It was this support and these outlets that would get me through any challenge I faced. It was the picture of normalcy that way. This picture of family life should sound familiar to you.

Where things take a turn is that my worldview from the start has always been from a different vantage point. Literally. I was always tiny due to a chromosomal abnormality. This abnormality also has left me unable to have children and with many medical conditions that require monitoring. From a young age, I was poked and prodded, but the doctors were stymied at my impaired growth. It wasn't until I was ten that a very astute doctor, who had heard about Turner Syndrome, decided to do a blood test that confirmed that I had the condition.

The medical community didn't really know a lot about Turner then, so my mother agreed to involve me in research when I was thirteen. I really wasn't one who blanched at having to do something new thanks to my mom. While I could get extremely anxious at first, I got used to facing things head-on. Mom made sure I understood that this research was voluntary, and that I didn't have to participate. Okay, she bribed me with a trip to Ocean City Maryland if I spent the few days in the hospital for more poking and prodding.

It was a little strange to be in the hospital and not be sick. I saw a lot of other children who were confined to their beds. I wasn't scared, just so homesick and bored! I had to keep an IV in my arm the whole time for the blood draws, but I could walk around the floor. I would pace at night until the nurses would play a game with me and get me back into bed. I remember my sisters' shocked looks after seeing my bruised arms (from the IVs). Periodic hospital and doctor visits, poking and prodding, being examined from head to toe were the norm for me through adolescence. When I would get impatient, my mother would sing me the song, "Show me the way to go home. I'm tired and I wanna go to bed..." Do you know that one? It was so silly, but it eventually made me laugh and relax. I still think of that song when I need to calm down.

Along with the medical issues, I have dealt most of my life with very low self-esteem. For a period of six years, from third grade until ninth grade, I was bullied in school because of my size. The total gamut of verbal taunts and physical assaults. I didn't want to fight, but I was often forced to defend myself. At home, I would lie awake most of the night anxious about confrontations I would face the next day. I became a perfectionist with schoolwork stressing over the slightest mistake. Hours upon hours I would pour over my books to get it 'just right'. Often, a slight mistake would bring me to a meltdown either in school or later at home. There was no policy regarding bullying in place at school then, like now, to stop this behavior. In ninth grade, it finally ended when my mother and I met with my biggest tormenter and she agreed that enough was enough. By then, I began second-guessing myself, and I became hesitant about making decisions without affirmation. Now you, like most high school-aged youth, may have found the transition to college and the adult world filled with angst and 'drama'. This time for me, however, became a turning point.

After attending a year at a college in North Carolina where I felt held back, I transferred to Emerson College in Boston where I thrived. I was in my element surrounded by like-minded peers. I could finally explore who I was without being laughed at or belittled as I studied theater and was on my own. I was cast in a traveling show that year, and I actually earned some money! It was exhilarating!

Then meeting my first husband again changed my life's course dramatically. We met in the Boston Commons, an open area along the Charles River. He was a lot older, and I was intrigued. I quickly found out, though, that he was smothering. He was constantly at my door asking to go out. When I had plans to spend time with a friend who was visiting, he still showed up with alcohol. I had just turned twenty-one and my friend was twenty! Yes, he was a smoker and a drinker, which was a turn-off. But I was hooked. I thought he was so charismatic and handsome. Our relationship for the next eleven years became a rollercoaster that never stopped. That lurch in the pit of my stomach was a constant, and I became an emotional mess. My life became all about taking care of his needs to keep him from lashing out.

I was living in an apartment on Charles Street when we met, and my roommate was moving out. He jumped at the chance to move in. Despite my trepidations, I agreed. It was the summer before my senior year. I was working and taking a couple of summer classes. He was working at a liquor store. It wasn't long before he became enmeshed in every aspect of my life. He had to be involved in everything I did, and I quickly became uncomfortable. My worst fears came true when many discussions led to him growing angry and physically holding me down, not letting me up until he was satisfied that I wouldn't contradict him. I remember distinctly one time he became enraged when we were walking in the Prudential Center and he threatened to shove my head through the glass. I ran and managed to get to our apartment and lock the door.

The typical pattern of abuse continued for eleven years. Turmoil, violence, making up. All I kept thinking was that I could deal with his behavior. I just had to accept it. I wasn't that naive that I thought I could change him. The 'drama' became normal. Crazy huh?

We moved to California shortly after I graduated from Emerson. My brother-in-law owned property and helped us find connections and get an apartment. It wasn't long before my ex's abusive behavior caught the attention of my sisters who eventually decided to intervene. They helped me move out one day while he was out of the apartment. It was humiliating and exactly what I didn't want to happen. My older sisters coming to my rescue and watching out for me. I was an adult, not a kid! I was twenty-three!

I thought his leaving was the end of the turmoil, but I was mistaken. One day (I'm not sure how much later), he showed up at the apartment with a suitcase. I only agreed to talk, but he decided he was moving back in. His domineering personality pulled me right back in again.

After the earthquake in San Francisco in 1989, we moved back to Pittsburgh. A friend of the family helped us by renting an apartment. Again, assistance from my family. My parents, despite the circumstances in California, decided to give my ex a second chance. It was short-lived. Throughout our relationship, he rarely worked, going from job to job. I always worked and supported us. I finally got a car in California, but of course, he mostly drove it. And wrecked it. And got a DUI. He even stole from my parents in Pittsburgh, and I *still* stayed with him! The culmination of all of this behavior and his out of control lifestyle was that he finally went to prison, though not for the DUI or anything related to alcohol.

For the next six months, I felt lost. I could hardly function. I worked and went through the day on autopilot. I honestly don't know how I got up and kept going during that time. I kept thinking that I had to work; I had to take care of my animals (I had four cats and three dogs). Despite the abuse, I couldn't bring myself to leave him. This was the first major relationship I had experienced. He had such a hold on me that I couldn't imagine my life any other way. I resigned myself to the fact that the volatility and abuse would just be something I would have to continue living with. My life still centered around him! We had been together for eleven years and married for four years by then. I was still paying—literally and figuratively. I would send him money, go visit him (driving four to five hours at first), and talk with the lawyer. But as time passed, my passion for theater reignited. I also went back to school, earning a Master's degree in Counseling Psychology. After a while, this achievement and being away from my ex's influence gave me the confidence I needed to break away once and for all. Now, I'm amazed. I used to pray to God for his freedom. Now I thank God he's not in my life anymore. He was released after ten years, recommitted a crime, and was imprisoned again. By then, my journey to healing, self-awareness, and growth had only just begun.

I have to take a step back now because between my husband being incarcerated and starting my journey as a counselor, I lost my job, and I had another life-altering experience that, happening when it did, really shaped my life as it is today. Three years after my husband went to prison, I went with my parents to visit family and friends in Florida. My mother had rented a car, and we were staying at my aunt's condo. My parents, aunt, and I had an enjoyable dinner with some of my aunt's friends one evening during the visit. After dinner, I remember being impatient with my father as we were getting back into the car. He needed assistance walking due to a stroke, so he was slow getting in. I walked to the other side of the car, and I got into the back seat on the driver's side. Little did I know that decision would save my life, but cost my aunt hers. On the way home, my mother pulled out onto the freeway to change directions, which is legal in Florida, and we were broadsided. Our car careened across the freeway. I was thrown against my aunt and then flung back to the other side hitting, cutting my chin on the window handle. My father and aunt were crushed and killed instantly. My mother was alert afterwards, hit by the airbag and taken to a nearby hospital. I was unconscious and life-flighted to a hospital in St. Petersburg eighty miles from the accident. I remember waking up in the helicopter and the crew telling me they were taking me to the hospital, and that my father and aunt had died.

At the hospital, my chin was stitched, and I was rushed around on a gurney to have multiple tests done. My sister later said that she spoke with me over the phone, but I don't even remember that conversation. It was like I was in a haze. I was numb and not thinking clearly.

After an evening of evaluation at the hospital, the staff decided I didn't need admitted and released me at 5 am the next morning. Still dressed in a thin hospital gown and booties, I signed the discharge papers and traveled eighty miles by cab to my aunt's house. Looking back, I can't believe that they let me leave. I kept saying that I wanted to get out of there, but my condition was precarious. I had just lost two relatives and suffered head trauma leaving me dazed and off-balance. What I felt was a lack of compassion from the hospital left me re-traumatized. I had at least expected hospital staff to stay with me until I could reach someone to pick me up, not to be released to a stranger to travel eighty miles in a hospital gown and booties. I later wrote them a three-page letter describing my experience and how they handled my situation. The chief of emergency sent me a response stating that multiple trained professionals had evaluated me and found no reason to admit me. Again, my plight was ignored. I felt worthless and devalued.

My aunt lived in a gated senior community, and once we arrived at her complex, the nice cab driver rang buzzers until a neighbor came out. This kind woman took one look at me and brought me inside. I told her about the accident and about the hospital where my mother was being kept. She called the hospital, and her husband went to pick up keys to my aunt's home. Meanwhile, my mother had spoken to one of my sisters and my aunt's sons. I later learned that her nurse was going to come to me to take me to my aunt's after her shift. No one could believe how I had left the hospital barely dressed. My sisters and cousins arrived in Florida later that day and took over. I went back home the next day.

A long healing process both physically and emotionally followed. I didn't take much time off, and I suffered from severe vertigo for a long time. I took off work initially for just the three bereavement days thinking I needed to just get back to my normal routine. The company I worked for wasn't too sympathetic. When it was time to return, it was all I could do to get out of bed. I would literally almost fall over from dizziness. It was like I was moving in quicksand. My thoughts were cloudy. I started seeing a chiropractor because it was painful to move my neck. He prescribed physical therapy. Weeks of appointments and physical exertion only made my fatigue increase. I eventually had bloodwork done for a non-related issue that showed that I had contracted Epstein Barr, an illness similar to mononucleosis. Okay, great! Here's another hurdle to tackle. The mental and physical fatigue reached a peak after this latest onslaught. I was crying constantly, and I could not keep up with housework or commitments. Within a year, I was fired from my job as mentioned previously.

To lose my job was actually a blessing because I was out of work for two months, and I was able to fully take the time to grieve and heal. The magnitude of almost losing my life was really starting to impact me, and the emotions were intense. I never felt anger or blamed my mother. Instead, I felt some survivor's guilt and the sense of having to give back. There was also a sense of peace as if my father and aunt were cheering me on and telling me that this was my chance to shine and to "live my life fully," which was actually a very comforting feeling. I didn't really know what "fully" meant at the time. I just knew how great it felt to just do what I wanted to do sometimes, not just what I felt I was expected to do all the time. I carried on at first because I wanted my father and aunt to be proud of me. Then, I carried on because I wanted more for myself. I wanted to show them that I would be okay. I wanted to honor them. I finally began to think that I deserved more than to live a life just getting by.

Back to why should you pay attention to this story. It's not just about overcoming physical limitations. It's more about maintaining emotional stability through life's challenges. Going to school for my masters was the best decision I made through those three years of enormous loss—it's a lot to lose a relationship, job, security, and survive an accident that killed family members. My classes brought back the feeling of empowerment and validated my healing process. I so needed intellectual stimulation! We were encouraged to engage in counseling to better understand what it's like to be on the receiving end. I decided to find a therapist and take another step toward my emotional growth. The poor therapist! She couldn't get a word in! I just couldn't stop talking. It was exhilarating to me to be able to express myself and not be rebuffed or laughed at. I only went for four sessions because she was leaving the practice. Just verbally talking things through was validating and helped me focus my thoughts and gain confidence. What I had to say actually mattered! I started dating again and found my now second husband, who is the complete antithesis of my first. Along the way, I discovered my voice and to trust my instincts. They have been rarely wrong. Mostly I learned that it's okay to make mistakes and not be "perfect." There is no such thing. Experience is subjective. Opinion is subjective. I've also learned that I needed to slow down. I can't do everything and be responsible for everything. Now I've been married for twelve and a half years to a wonderful man, work at two private practices in my field of study as well as counsel cyber students online. I even took a chance and started a theater group with a partner and collaborated in compiling this book (okay, so maybe I haven't slowed down that much). No, it isn't always easy. I'm not always sure where things will take me, but I do know that whatever life brings now, I have the grounding and trust in myself to persevere. So, dear reader, I share this story publicly to offer you support and encouragement. To show you that it is possible to persevere and overcome very tough situations. No matter what choices you have made to this point, nothing is set in stone. You can correct mistakes. You don't have to spin your wheels seeking perfection. Just reach for achieving the best possible outcome. After reading my story, how will you live your life? Will you live in defeat, hate, regret, and fear or in triumph, love, pride, and confidence? It's your choice.

Co-authored and Compiled by Jacqueline Rech

Ellen Ulmer, LPC, NCC, NAADC

Ellen Ulmer is a licensed professional counselor, nationally certified counselor, and certified advanced drug and alcohol counselor working in private practice in Pittsburgh, PA. She received a Bachelor of Science in Theater Performance from Emerson College in Boston, MA, and a Master of Science in Counseling Psychology from Chatham College (University) in Pittsburgh, PA. Prior to working in private practice, Ellen worked as a drug and alcohol counselor for Discovery House (a Methadone Maintenance program), Gateway Rehab, and Pyramid Healthcare. She has also worked as a care manager for Lifespan, an agency that assists seniors with gaining access to county programs and as a student assistance liaison in Pittsburgh schools. She currently works with a variety of clients from children to seniors who face a multitude of issues including anxiety, depression, behavioral problems, life transitions, and substance use/addiction. She lives with her husband, Steven, and cat, Kedi

CHAPTER THREE:

Permission to be a Human

Lauren Falgout, LCSW, MPHIL, CCTP

When I sat down to tell my story, my mind simultaneously went blank and was flooded with a million ways to start. On the forefront of my mind was the vulnerability I felt in telling my story and fearing the reaction of others who might read it. But then my husband, Jeremy, sat me down and said, *"Lauren don't you ever be embarrassed by your story. Your past makes you who you are, and your struggles make you that much greater at what you do."* This was the reminder I knew, but needed to hear, just one more time. His words hold true for me, and anyone reading this who might need a Jeremy in their life too.

First, let me introduce myself. My name is Lauren Falgout, and currently, I am a licensed clinical social worker. I work at a local college and at a private practice in my community. I have multiple degrees in the field of social work and psychology. I am a suicide awareness activist and speaker. I speak at colleges, at trainings for peer professionals, and engage in other educational and motivational speaking events. I specialize in happiness, self-care, and suicide… what a trio. I can go on and on about how I may look on paper, which all matter, but the real accomplishment is being alive. I hope my journey and chapter sheds light on the grit needed, and the ability to, grow through darkness and give courage to challenge mental health and any prior stigma it may hold for you. The goal of this chapter is to allow you a window into my past, and to provide optimism and hope for your future. So, it is with warmth, and acceptance that I welcome you!

Let's start at the very beginning. I lived the ideal American dream, literally. I am the middle-born among my two sisters, and we were raised our whole childhood into adulthood in the same large house, with loving parents who fully supported our interests in any aspects of life. I had, and still have, a great group of core friends, was involved in dance, cheerleading, and track, and was always going on incredible family vacations. I was outgoing and active, and my family always provided abundant emotional, spiritual, and financial support. I was happy, well cared for, blessed, and lacked for nothing.

I made my first attempt to kill myself when I was sixteen years old. This by no means was my first plan to end my life, but it was the first impulsive attempt after an emotionally charged day. It wasn't the last time either. I can still remember it like yesterday. Sitting in my room, my entire wonderful family downstairs, blasting Linkin Park and deciding it was my time to go. I was in *pain* and I wanted the pain to go away. Thankfully I did not die that day. I did, however, scare the shit out of myself. I covered my attempt up, and to this day, my family has no idea (Guess I covered everything up back then—hiding the pain this well didn't give anyone a chance to help me).

I continued to cut myself, use maladaptive coping mechanisms, hide behind lies, battle eating disorders, depression, and anxiety, and struggled with suicidal thoughts, intent, and ideations all throughout high school and college. This wasn't always linear; life would ebb and flow and it would creep back in extreme ways. I was lost, a shell of who I am now, and could barely recognize myself. I did not believe I would make it past twenty-one years old; at the time I did not see a point.

Let's fast forward to today. Now I am twenty-nine and married to an incredible man who is also a therapist. We have two fur babies and just bought our dream home. I am working my dream job as a therapist, and love it so much that it doesn't feel like work. And not to toot my own horn, but I think I'm pretty good at it. I still have incredible friends, family, and feel loved daily. I get out of the house to spend time with these friends, go to CrossFit every day, travel, read, am in pursuit of my doctorate, and take part in a plethora of fun activities with incredible people. I spend my mornings singing, talking to my dogs, and dancing. I am happy. I am lucky. I am blessed. My life has purpose and I genuinely love it.

Yet, I still wake up with an indescribable heaviness, sometimes. I still struggle with insomnia, sometimes. I still want to cry myself to sleep for no apparent reason sometimes. I still get bad anxiety episodes and chew my nails to the bone sometimes. I still struggle with anger sometimes. I still have negative self-talk, and passive death wishes sometimes. And if I didn't continue to care for and check-in with myself every day, I would struggle even more than I do, and I would find myself in the same boat I was in back in high school. *These things don't control me anymore but that doesn't mean they don't still try.*

The stigma of who depression preys on is a barrier to overcoming it. Depression doesn't give a shit that I have three, almost four, degrees in the field of psychology. Depression doesn't care that I've overcome it before. Depression does not care what you have done, or who you are. It attacks *all humans* equally. The second I forget this is the second I become susceptible.

You know about the idealistic parts of my childhood and where I am today, but I'd like to fill in the blanks a bit. I will not go into too much detail as, even if I did, no one's story or struggle is the same. But I can tell you all about the self-hatred; then and now. Those irrational, yet strong, thoughts that monopolize your mind. I can tell you what it's like to hold the stereotype of being 'the happy silly friend' in one breath, and wanting with all your power to be dead in the next. That duality of two people inside of you is exhausting. I can tell you what it's like coming from an incredible family and constantly punishing myself with the thought of, *You have no reason to be depressed you have a good life.* Now the thoughts are, *Lauren you have a great life; you do this for a living you have no reason to be depressed.* I have to battle this stigma about mental health constantly. It was harder then, asking how could I, the social butterfly with a great family, great grades, and great friends wake up and want to die every single day? But I did. I can tell you all about the times I'd be sitting on the bathroom floor, sobbing, back against the wall, praying for the pain to end, saying nasty things about myself and feeling alone. That emptiness is haunting. I can tell you about staring at myself in the mirror and in great detail picking apart every single physical attribute I possessed until all that was left are feelings of disgust. This tedious scrutiny is heavy, persistent, and inescapable.

I still do sometimes.

Because that's depression. Depression plays no favorites and just because you check all the boxes of a culturally ideal life doesn't mean it magically skips over you. It took me over two decades to learn this. All through high school and college I cut myself, disliked myself, struggled with depression, was angry, engaged in maladaptive coping mechanisms, and tried to kill myself behind closed doors. *I tried to question how I was feeling and deny it instead of accepting my depression and working on it.*

I cannot tell you the number of times I wrote suicide notes with every intent to use them as a final goodbye.

I cannot tell you the number of times I tried to take my own life.

I cannot tell you the number of times I would sneak away from dinner to rid myself of the food I ate.

I cannot tell you the number of times I woke up disappointed, wishing I was dead in a deep sadness.

I cannot tell you the number of days I was scared of life in general. I have lost count of the number of times I would lie and say I was fine when inside I was screaming.

I cannot tell you how many nights I spent crying on the bathroom floor.

I cannot tell you the number of times I have cut myself.

I cannot tell you how heavy it was to carry pain, shame, anger, and sadness around all the time.

I cannot tell you the number of times I survived … but I did. I woke up and kept going.

I became a therapist because my own experiences helped me understand the importance of mental health, and the difference a caring and compassionate therapist can make. That's why most of us become therapists, in my opinion. This field is driven less by money and more by passion and compassion. When I was fifteen, my mother took me to see a therapist for a short time. Her name was Molly and, while I never told her, she saved my life. She planted the seed I needed to grow. I fully believe without this struggle I would not have the life I have and adore now. Mental health disorders are not like the common cold that go away in seven days with a z-pack. Depression doesn't disappear—we just get *stronger*. I would never have become a therapist, moved around, went on to higher education, or found the things I enjoy now. Without my history, and the tools I needed to put into place to grow, I would not have found who I was; so, I am grateful.

When I read the paragraphs I just wrote, it seems like I am describing two completely different people. But they're both me, and I am okay with that. I am proud of it, actually. I can be both depressed and happy. I can be both depressed and growing. I can be both depressed and a great therapist. Now I look back at my struggles, low points, and growth and feel strong, capable, and powerful. So, the question is, what got me from actively wanting to kill myself to coping with passive death wishes in a healthy way? What got me from throwing up my food, and hating my body to accepting who I am? What got me from hiding my depression, and allowing it to fester to openly sharing about my feelings? There are many things I *need* to incorporate in my day, every day, to help maintain balance between those two people I described. I will share a few of those things with you. By no means is this an exhaustive list. And it might look differently for you based on your talents, strengths, and interests.

- Of these things came my own journey of self-acceptance and growth. I learned to journal. I still journal every day. I write the positive things I did, positive quotes I read, or positive YouTube videos that motivate me to push and grow. I spend time with *gratitude* here. I reflect on my mood, my goals, my progress, and my power to persevere. This journal gave me perspective, gratitude, and positivity. This helped me see that being positive and happy didn't mean 'rainbows and butterflies everyday'; it meant seeing the positive even when things are negative and having confidence that I could be okay through it and keep it in check.

- I surround myself with people who impact my life in a positive way and support my growth. There is a saying that says, "You become like the people you spend most of your time with. Choose wisely." A big part of this growth was to care for my mental and emotional health by putting distance between myself and toxic people who made me feel less than deserving of the healing I fight for every day. Even if that toxic person was *me*. That was so hard. The realization that I could not continue to grow in healthy ways while maintaining relationships or friendships with these people was hard to accept. I reminded myself that just because I had these relationships for years did not mean I had to keep them in my life. I read something somewhere that really stuck with me and supported that thought, it said, "If a person is costing you your peace of mind, they are costing you too much." I urge you to let go of those negative relationships and friendships so you can grow. This step helped me branch away from a version of myself I did not like to create space and energy to grow.

- Healthy hobbies were a game-changer for me as well. I have always enjoyed physical fitness and athletics. Running saved my life as a kid, and all through college. Now, I joined CrossFit and it gives me something much more than just fitness. Working with a fun group of supportive individuals every day boosted my mood and sense of community. Focusing on the pounds I could lift or push became more important than the pounds I saw on the scale. I realized a strong body that could help me through life was more important than a body focused on the exchange of calories. I joke sometimes that CrossFit saved my life, but I'm not so sure it really is a joke. Because the bottom line is that being social daily, learning to mentally prepare for a hard workout helps me mentally prepare for a hard day, being physically active every day, and belonging to a community working together towards similar goals, was invaluable to my healing process. *Thank you MET and AR Strength.*

- Getting the most of my day. There are twenty-four hours available to every person and I decided I wanted to access as many as possible in a healthy way. For me, solely for my needs and schedule, I wake up every day at 4:30 am. Waking up early gives me an hour every day to spend quiet time with the dogs, prep for my workday, check-in on my mood, and allows me time to adjust and show kindness to myself. This precious sixty-minute window at the beginning of my day gives me a chance to organize myself inside and out and, based upon my mood, put into place daily activities to cope with where I am. There is a saying that goes, "If you win the first hour of the day, you win the whole day." I believe it to be true. Find your calm each day. Make time for you and the things that matter. This step gives me serenity and time to control the things within my control each day.

- Mindfulness plays another big part in my daily recovery. What kind of therapist would I be if I didn't promote the power of mindfulness? It may seem cliché but my ability to be aware without judgment in all activities, from my mood, to my eating, to my decisions makes all the difference. Being mindful helped me make better choices with food, without acting on emotion-based thoughts, and in taking accountability so I could grow. This awareness without judgement is freeing.

- I gained the ability to accept that I will feel down and depressed, and with that ability came the freedom to advocate for my needs. Learning to say "no" and put boundaries into place was initially extremely hard and ridden with guilt. This meant RSVP'ing 'no' to a reunion, a night out, a wedding, or a baby shower so I could rebalance myself. This also meant asking from others and expressing my limits. A quote I saw by Silvy Khoucasian that was impactful here was, "Empathy without boundaries is self-destruction." Read that again. And again, if you have to. We are trained in this field to harness and perfect our empathy skills. However, the other half of that is keeping empathy in check with self-care.

For example, this week has been hectic and draining between long hours at work, the nature of our work, protecting myself from being triggered by clients expressing suicidal thoughts, writing my dissertation, and the chaos of life in general. After a twelve-hour day yesterday, I had to check in with myself and used mindfulness to notice the feelings of being heavy and down. I was able to ask my husband to go to the park with me for a walk. Some days I tell him I need to go for a run. Other days I've spent so much energy listening and being present in so many powerful therapy sessions, I have had to ask my husband to give me complete silence when I get home. It's important to check in with yourself, discover your needs, and ask for time away from others to care for yourself. It is okay to ask for and get the help you need when you need it. Set boundaries. This step helps me find the confidence to no longer be a prisoner of shame and put myself and my needs in the forefront of my schedule.

It is okay to seek help. It is okay to talk about it—even if it makes other people uncomfortable. READ THIS AGAIN! And AGAIN! Read it until you give yourself permission. There are still times I will share about my suicide attempts, or my depression, and am instantly met with a look of sheer shock, confusion, and disbelief. *This is okay.* This is my chance to educate others, and in doing so break the mold they may currently have of what a person struggling with mental health issues looks like. This paves the way for others.

The difference between my life then and now is the acceptance and grace I give myself. I will repeat this again: Depression does not care that I am a therapist, I will always be a human first. This means I need to grant myself permission to be a human. Now I take the time to sit with myself and ask how I feel. I accept that sometimes I am going to feel down and will require a little extra care on my part. No one will do this for me, so I have to stir up discipline and make the changes I deserve. Sometimes, after a client leaves, I spend time reflecting on the session to discover if any part of it was triggering and why; because it has been in the past and it will be in the future. It's okay as a therapist to seek supervision for those times, or to continue to see your own therapist. It's okay to drive home feeling a little overwhelmed and then put into place the tools I have developed to work through those feelings, rather than sweep them under the rug. Most importantly I place my physical, emotional, and mental health care first so that I can be more present and empathic with my clients. It took me years to get here but I made it. Accepting where I am every day, making changes, and being open to help is crucial. If I am not functioning at my best in all levels, then my clients are being robbed of my best, and that could be a dangerous thing for all of us. I still make mistakes. I still fall down. That is okay. Now I allow myself to stumble and help myself back up. In this profession, something that gives me comfort is knowing that just because a doctor calls out sick doesn't mean he's a bad doctor, it means he is human. His medical degree doesn't mean he is magically immune to all medical issues. For me, this means it's okay for me as a therapist to call out for a mental health day, or to work through feeling depressed, or to be otherwise emotionally or mentally down. These instances don't make me a bad therapist, they make me human. And I fully accept my own humanity. Allow yourself to be human. Allow yourself to grow. Allow yourself to make a change. Allow yourself to feel the highs and lows that come with being who you are. Never be ashamed of what makes you who you are. Your depression is not a sign of weakness; it shows true strength. You deserve healing, you deserve happiness, and you certainly deserve peace of mind. Take care of yourself; you are so very important and you, whoever you are, deserve more. This is scary and hard to navigate sometimes. I will leave you with one last quote, there is a saying I like to remind myself of quite often, "Feel the fear and do it anyway." I guess my bottom line here is, keep going even when it feels impossible, choose yourself, choose happiness, have self-love, create time for self-care, and have self-acceptance because you are deserving of it all even when it feels unbearable. This is what helped me put my depression into check and take back my life.

Your life belongs to *you*. Regardless who you are, what your life was prior, and your story thus far. A diagnosis does not define you. A job title doesn't hinder you from seeking help. You still have a right to sit in your feelings, own them, overcome hardship, reach out for a helping hand, and build the life you want. Find 'wholeness' because this is a tool to finding happiness. Wholeness is constant. Forgive yourself for being human and grow into something indescribably strong.

Jackie shared a quote with me by Juilette Lewis that said, "The bravest thing I ever did was continue my life when I wanted to die"

Thank you for reading my story.

Co-authored and Compiled by Jacqueline Rech

Lauren Falgout, LCSW, MPHIL, CCTP

Lauren Falgout is a licensed clinical social worker. Lauren completed her Bachelor's Degree in Psychology from Penn State University (B.A.), a Master's Degree in Social Work at University of Southern California (M.S.W), a second Master's Degree in Psychological Research at Walden University (MPHIL), certified clinical trauma professional (CCTP), and is currently in pursuit of her Doctorate in General Psychology through Walden University. She is currently in the dissertation phase of her degree and is highly interested in exercise aids for mental health concerns and stress.

Lauren excels in a variety of therapy techniques including motivational interviewing, dialectical behavioral therapy, person-centered care, trauma-informed care, experiential therapy, and cognitive behavioral therapy. She currently works in a private practice seeking a wide array of mental health needs across a wide array of client populations. Lauren speaks publicly about self-care, happiness, suicide awareness, and depression. She works in a therapy and professor role at a college. Lauren is a large supporter of mental health. Her free time is filled with spending time with family, her husband, friends, exercising, and caring for her two big dogs!

CHAPTER FOUR:

Broken Together

Michelle E. Tanner, MEd, NCC, LPC

We start out as a beautifully crafted clay pot—indestructible, purposeful, ready to bring happiness to ourselves and to someone else. At that time, we meet our special someone, and a seed is planted. With proper care, a flower starts to blossom and thrive—our soul is singing. Then, trouble comes, and we are angrily hurled onto the floor only to shatter into a thousand tiny pieces—each shard telling its own painful saga. Other times, we are taken away from the sunlight, placed in a dark corner on a shelf, and forgotten about. The flower begins to wither, and eventually, die, to only become an ugly shriveled up weed with no more purpose.

These are my two relationship stories—one of abuse and one of neglect.

Who we are in relationships reveals a lot about ourselves, and it's typically when problems arise, or the relationship ends, when some ugly truths are revealed. Yet, there is hope for redemption and rebirth.

The Narcissist Abuser

First, let me introduce you to the narcissist abuser. I met him through a mutual friend, and at first, I couldn't stand him. He was loud, obnoxious, and opinionated while also being a heavy smoker, drinker, potty mouth, and gambler. With how I just described him, you will probably be shocked to learn that, months later, when he asked me out for a drink, I accepted. It would take a few months, but I would come to discover that my curiosity would nearly kill me. Once there, and after about an hour of catching up, he told me that he was really into me and asked what it would take for me to give him a chance. He was charming and determined to be a part of my life. The codependent hiding inside of me was pleased and ready for the challenge.

During the early part of our relationship, he was great, following through with everything he initially promised. But, as time went on, the façade was abandoned. I met the narcissist abuser. I took the verbal abuse for a while. He would say, "You better be doing something when I get home from work and not sitting on the couch watching TV," followed by always expecting dinner served to him on the couch, etc. If I didn't do something to his liking, or if he was simply in a bad mood, I'd hear, "You whore! You are the dumbest person I know. I can't believe you're a teacher," and many worse things. I was a victim in my own home. My flower was withering, and I felt my sacred clay pot becoming less indestructible.

It all came to a head one horrifying night. He wanted to go out drinking and take my car. I was already upset about this because he had no license due to multiple DUIs, but there was no saying "no" to him. Later that night, I was downstairs doing laundry, and I heard him stumble in the door. A whirlwind of anger and fear overtook me because he chose to drive home drunk in *my* car, and I knew how he got when he drank. My heart was racing as I was responding to a friend's text, and while I was doing so, he came downstairs. In his drunken stupor, he assumed I was texting another guy and began yelling, demanding that I show him who I was texting. I lightly tossed my phone to him, but it accidentally hit him on the chin. Thinking that I was trying to purposefully hit him, he became violent. As I'm writing this, I'm replaying the scene in slow motion in my head. His towering frame came hurtling toward me accompanied by pure hatred on his face. There was no escape. He pinned me against a door, and at that moment, I was trembling in fear not sure what was to come. He raised his fist, and I felt the breeze from it on my ear as his fist blasted a hole through the door. I remained calm. He let me go, stormed upstairs while swearing and saying heart-wrenching things, and what did I do? I continued to do laundry. I held it together because I *had* to. I knew that if I chose to do anything else at that moment, more violence would follow, and I was scared. Finally, I went upstairs to put the laundry away, and he followed me into the room continuing to say heinous things. I ignored him, and that infuriated him more. Out of the corner of my eye, I saw his long arm coming at me as he picked me up by the neck and pinned me against the wall. At that moment, I thought my life was over.

Miraculously, and there's no other word to describe it, he broke down in tears, dropped me, and hurried out of the house. The pot fell to the ground and shattered into a million little pieces—each sliver representing every harsh word, every violent act, and every time I should have left, but didn't. The lifeless flower and soil spilling out onto the floor. I was broken. Exposed. I did not have it all together. As I fell to the floor sobbing for several hours, it was at that moment when my heart hardened toward him. It was also the moment when I felt Jesus pull me to his chest and allow me to sob in his loving arms. I was flooded with his compassion, mercy, love, and grace.

Over the next few weeks, I ended my relationship and started attending church again. Sure, it took a year for me to fully forgive the abuser and move on with my life, but I did it. With prayer, reading the Bible, attending church, and surrounding myself with other Christians, shards of my pot were glued back together, until I felt whole and ready to replant a new flower. I *thought* the glue in my pot was strong enough when I met my now-ex-husband.

The Avoider

Painful silence … the only words to describe how it felt sitting in my divorce attorney's office, waiting for him to arrive. In the quietness, my negative self-talk rang louder and louder…you are a failure, failure, FAILURE! I couldn't silence my inner voice, and I began to cry. With each dropped tear, memories of how I failed came flooding back. "Compose yourself, Michelle," I had to tell myself. The attorney came into the room, and the consultation began as I sorted through assets and completing the divorce paperwork. I was broken ... again! I was the neglected pot holding a dying flower. This is what happens when the proper love and work isn't present in a marriage. So, I ended up there, in that divorce attorney's office, filling out forms about division of assets.

Rewind to the beginning. When I first saw him, I thought to myself, *Who's that guy?* Even though I thought his style was a little dorky, he piqued my interest. A couple of weeks later, I ran into him, and we ended up in a deep discussion about life. He showed himself to be compassionate, expressed his desire to serve others, and had a strong heartbeat for the Lord. Compared to my last ex, this one seemed too good to be true. I was hooked! Soon after, we started talking on social media, hanging out in a small group, and eventually, I worked up the courage to invite him over to watch a movie. I became the pursuer.

After several dates, he handed me a letter. The letter talked about how much he loved me, how he knew what he wanted, no matter what outsiders thought, etc. My flower was more vibrant than ever- I thought I had found the ONE! Our relationship moved pretty quickly; everything was happening so fast with a quick engagement and marriage. I was in the middle of pursuing my education and didn't notice just how much I didn't know about this person who had captured my heart.

The typical honeymoon phase of marriage lasts for the first six months to a year, and ours lasted about three months. It was an uphill battle of him withdrawing to his fantasy world to escape his personal demons and my love addiction, mixed with should haves and could haves, rigidity, stubbornness, near-absence of intimacy, lack of respect, and the list continues. We struggled. God sent people to speak to our lives to tell us to go to marriage counseling, and we ignored all of them. We tried to fix our issues ourselves, and our faults ended up playing off each other. We found ourselves in a vicious cycle of bargaining and blame. In our short five-year marriage, my husband asked for two 'separations' to reflect, process, read the Bible, and pray to see what he really wanted. The first separation was during Christmas, and the second time was a year or so later, around my thirtieth birthday and Valentine's Day. So, not only did I feel utter rejection, but this rejection took place on special occasions. However, we kept pushing forward without any real resolutions.

Even though the marriage wasn't sturdy, we still discussed having children. My flower started to regain some health and color. In preparation, we bought a bigger house and a bigger car. He went along with all these plans, all while keeping his intention of leaving me a secret. With one rejection of intimacy after another, I realized something deeper was going on with my husband, and a few months after discussing children, on our five-year anniversary, I heard the dreadful words—*I want a divorce*. I was overcome with feelings of anger and a sense of betrayal. I felt led on by his promises of a future with me, and I felt abandoned, especially on such a milestone.

Ironically, we still tried marriage counseling, and after several sessions, we both acknowledged that it wasn't working—we were *finally* on the same page about the finality of our relationship. It wasn't until he moved out when my world truly felt like it was falling apart. My pot started cracking as I felt shame, anger, rejection, failure, depression, a loss of identity, and loneliness. I knew God was there, but I had so many questions. How did I get here? Why did God allow this to happen? I was raised in a pastor's family, and divorce was never an option. I was taught the biblical principles of marriage and how to serve my husband. Not only was I judging myself, but I also got the looks in church and heard the whispers and rumors: *What happened? Did one of them cheat? He's too good of a guy, so it had to be her fault.* Those rumblings tore me to shreds because I couldn't believe that church people could look at someone hurting and in need, yet choose gossip instead of love. I wanted to shout my truth from the rooftops!

During this grieving process, I tried to stay as busy as possible because I thought that was the answer, but, really, *I* became the avoider. Then, I endured a serious knee injury and was immobile for several weeks. How ironic, right? I wanted to avoid facing my internal injuries, so God allowed an external injury to provide the perfect atmosphere to deal with it all at once. It was in this period of stillness when my work began, and it was later finished in counseling. Through counseling, I was able to reflect on two of my past failed relationships, and I learned many valuable lessons.

The Glue

It was essential for me to address the feelings of abandonment and those surrounding broken promises to God, lost identity, and the grieving process. After dealing with my abuser, I thought that immersing myself in church would be enough, but I learned the hard way that, personally, I needed counseling too. When I found a Christian counselor, everything started to make sense. I felt too betrayed and lonely during the marriage to allow myself to see that I also needed to accept some responsibility for why it ended. I wish I could write something different and say that our marriage was restored, but I can't. What I can say is that I identified two things about myself that, once addressed, helped me to become that indestructible flowerpot once again.

The Love Addict

A love addict's biggest fear is abandonment or rejection. The addict is also obsessed with being 'in love', and if that feeling isn't there, the addict creates, pulling from cognitive behavioral therapy, an irrational thought that there's something wrong with the relationship followed by the feeling of rejection, all leading to the behavior—usually something destructive like passive-aggressiveness. That obsession with being in love is what caused me to rush into commitment time and time again. Also, during my marriage, when my husband chose his fantasy world instead of intimacy with me, the repeated rejection drove me to flood my mind with many irrational thoughts: he doesn't love me anymore; he isn't attracted to me anymore, and there's something wrong with me. I felt more and more alone with each rejection of intimacy. We didn't know how to cope with our own issues, so he turned to isolating himself, and I turned to passive-aggressiveness. The more he isolated, the more critical I became of even the smallest flaws or infractions, thus, withholding the respect that he needed. Thankfully, my therapist was able to identify this unhealthy pattern within my past relationships and provided me with healthy coping strategies. Now, I am okay with and thrive in being alone. With hard work, I have created healthy boundaries for myself personally and within relationships.

The Codependent

Codependency was a term I learned and identified with, so much so that I committed to reading *Codependent No More: How to Stop Controlling Others and Start Caring for Yourself*. I quickly learned that I was a fixer. In the past, I was drawn to men that needed some sort of rescuing, as the case with my abuser. A part of my healing was to embrace detaching from people and their problems. Learning to say no was essential. I also needed to distinguish between my soul and my spirit, allowing myself not to react emotionally but to allow God's word to guide me.

The Refurbished Pot

My healing journey, though long, was one combined with my faith and counseling. Without God and therapy, I would still be sitting—stuck—in that painful silence…in a mess of a broken pot with soil, shards of clay, and a wilted flower scattered about. God allowed me to go through these experiences for a reason, and I choose to focus on giving God glory. I needed to stop allowing my past and other's reactions to define me and to restore my identity in Christ *alone*.

Yes, the pot was once broken, but God thoughtfully crafted it back together, with each piece telling a story of His love, affirmation, and promises as well as a renewed identity in Him. He made beauty from the ashes so that a new flower can be grown. *I am redeemed.*

And guess what? Redemption is there for you too—yes you! If you feel like you're trapped in a relationship with a narcissist or you're in a codependent relationship, there are warning signs. I missed them early on, but use my story to help you do what's best for YOU. Look for the arrogance, manipulation, selfishness, patronization, and demanding words. Watch out for the back-and-forth between their "need" for you and your "need" to help them out of their situation. If this sounds familiar, learn to put yourself first, set boundaries, and detach from the entanglement! You *are* strong, capable, and worth so much more, and you want to know something else? They can do it on their own too. I have faith in you! I am cheering for you! Start watering your flower so that it can blossom again.

Michelle E. Tanner, MEd, NCC, LPC

Michelle, professor and author, is a full-time professor at St. Bonaventure University while also on as adjunct faculty at a few other schools. Before academia, Michelle was a school counselor for three years, a middle school English teacher for nine years, and she is currently a licensed professional counselor in Pennsylvania.

Professionally, Michelle has a handful of publications and presentations on topics related to counseling. She is presently completing a doctoral program at Duquesne University in counselor education and supervision. Her passion is the holistic wellness model of counseling, particularly focusing on spirituality.

"The part can never be well unless the whole is well." —Plato, trans. 1901

CHAPTER FIVE:

Breaking Stigma

Patrick McElwaine, PsyD

My hope is that my life can help break stigma and motivate and inspire others. Here is my story.

The Early Days

I grew up in a row home in Northeast Philadelphia, Pennsylvania. My father was a Philadelphia fireman and my mother was a stay-at-home mom. I am the oldest of three children. My sister Melissa is two years younger than me and my brother Steven is five years younger. All in all, we had a great childhood. My parents were loving and caring, and we were happy! Those are the memories that I have for the first nine years of my life. Life seemed simple and fun, no worries at all. Who would have thought that on our summer vacation this simple and fun life would take an unfortunate turn?

Tragedy

On my ninth birthday, we took a family vacation to the Poconos in Pennsylvania. Our usual family vacation was a week down the Jersey shore; however, this summer my parents decided to go to the Pocono Mountains. We did the normal vacation stuff. There was a pool with a slide which was a lot of fun. We played with other children at the resort, went out to eat, and went to local tourist attractions. I remember playing basketball with my dad on the court near our cabin. On July 17th, I was playing tag with my brother, sister, and other children from the resort. I remember my dad walking up to me and asking if I wanted to go for a walk with him, but I told him I would rather keep playing with my friends.

The next morning, my siblings and I were still in bed when the resort manager came into our room. I remember her telling us that something happened to our dad. I am not sure if she told us he passed away; she may have, because I remember my sister and brother leaving the room while I turned away from her to look out the window and started to cry. I remember the sun hitting me on the face. When I got up to leave, it felt like everything was in slow motion; the room was filled with police and strangers. My mom came over and hugged me.

While we were spending time at the pool that week, my dad would make comments to my mom that he would love to go down the slide, but was embarrassed to do it in front of the guests. The curvy slide was the main attraction, and we loved it.

My dad was a guy who could make friends very easily with people he met. He was charismatic, social, and just an overall great guy. It is believed that the night of July 17th, as he went on his walk, he met up with a family we had befriended that week and had some beers with them. On the way back to our room, we believe that since there was no one around he decided to go down the slide, since we were leaving the following day. It is presumed that he swallowed water, panicked, and drowned. Around 11:00 pm that night, the police report said that someone heard choking and coughing but did not look to see. The toxicology showed that my dad had about six beers that night. He also had some clothing folded up on a chair near the pool as well as two Budweiser beers in a brown bag.

In one night, my entire world changed. My mom became a single mom with three children ages nine, six, and three. I remember playing at my dad's funeral, not understanding what was going on at all. I remember the Philadelphia Fire Department being extremely supportive to my mom during that year and many years after. I remember driving in the car one day and my mom commented that the car in front of us had my dad's favorite numbers (he played the lottery). My mom said that was a sign that he was still with us. I remember feeling good when she said that. The days, months, and years to follow were difficult but my mom did everything she could to make sure her children were physically, emotionally, and mentally good. For me, the first Christmas was the time when it hit me that my dad was gone forever. I realized that I would never see my dad again. I missed him so much! Sadness, heartbreak, and fear set in. My mom was there to comfort and love me through this time.

My Teenage Years

Entering my teenage years, I became more aware of the role that alcohol played with my dad's death, as well as his struggles with managing his alcohol use. My dad never sought treatment, but did try to stop his drinking on his own. In my early teen years, I was against drinking. I would tell my mom about my friends drinking each night when I got home. Then that stopped telling her about my friend because I started to drink when I was fifteen years old. I was a teenager who lost his father at an early age, was bullied, and had low self-esteem. They say that people get liquid courage from alcohol. I felt that it gave me liquid courage, confidence, and high self-esteem. I was able to talk to girls, go on dates, feel good about myself, and stick up for myself. I got into my first major fist-fight at fifteen when I saw an older kid bothering a younger kid. I felt great after that fight, reinforcing all the 'gifts' alcohol had given me. Everything in my life revolved around drinking.

When I graduated high school and then went on to college, I was able to get average grades while my partying and alcohol use increased. I was drinking and driving a lot and had many near accidents. My relationships were deteriorating because of alcohol but I still had some people who told me I did not have a drinking problem, so I listened to them rather than listen to those who tried to help me. At twenty years old, I was diagnosed with a fatty liver.

My doctor talked to me about how alcohol can harm the body. For six months, I stopped drinking and focused on my health. I believed I proved I did not have a problem. Then just like my dad, I treated myself to a six-pack of beer on vacation and was back at it again, stronger than ever.

Stages of Change

A few years later, I began a new job as a therapist at a residential treatment facility. That was where I met my future wife. I thought it was love at first sight, and I won her over with my charm. We started dating and early on I felt my drinking would end the relationship. I hurt her many times because of my drinking and ultimately decided to stop drinking again, but this time I knew I could not stop on my own. I began attending Alcoholics Anonymous meetings and therapy. My first day in recovery was June 23rd, 2005. I did not engage in recovery for myself; I started my recovery because I did not want to lose my girlfriend. But I became a chronic relapser.

When I wanted to hide my drinking from everyone, I began using pain killers and benzodiazepines. This way I could get the same feeling as being drunk and messed up, but no one would smell alcohol on me. The lies, deceit, reckless behavior, hurt and pain that I caused my family increased. I had passive thoughts of suicide where I didn't care about myself. During a long sober stretch, I got married, but my sober stretch did not last. Sometimes, I was genuine about wanting to stop my alcohol and drug use; other times I told people what they wanted to hear. How could I let go of the one thing that gave me confidence and increased my self-esteem and assertiveness? If people really loved me, they would accept me for my drinking and drug use instead of giving me a hard time, boundaries, and consequences. However, I could see that the road I was taking would eventually lead to my downfall and death.

Recovery

My personal and professional life was falling apart. I was on the verge of losing my wife, my career, and my life. After another significant mess, I started my recovery journey again.

On February 12, 2009, I went to another AA meeting to begin recovery again.

A week later, I met with a new psychiatrist for a therapy session. I was not nervous while sitting in the waiting room. I believe it was because I 'knew' I was not going to connect with the doctor. When our session began, I shared that I was a die-hard Eagles fan. He responded by saying he was not a football fan. Bad start already. Then I went through my story with him, one I have told many times before. I ended my story with, "Why does this keep happening to me?" He said, "I know why!" I was happy to hear this; I was waiting for his magical answer to help me stay clean and sober. He looked and pointed a finger at me and said, "Because you're an alcoholic and a drug addict!" He said this about eight different times during the session. That is all I could remember. I left pissed off and wanted to hurt him. I called my wife and told her, "You're not going to believe this but the first time I meet this guy, he points a finger at me and tells me I am a drug addict and alcoholic. I am a therapist; I know you're supposed to build a therapeutic relationship and I am supposed to like him." She responded with words I will never forget. "You might want to take a closer look at why you are so angry with him." I responded to that like a mature adult; I cursed at her and threw the phone down. But then I had my aha moment: I HATE that label; I did not want to be called an alcoholic or drug addict. I wanted it to go away, I did not want to be in treatment for it; how could treatment work when I was ashamed of these labels? I wondered if people would treat me differently if they found out I was an alcoholic and drug addict?

After that session, I continued to go to therapy and AA meetings. I continued to struggle with my treatment, but I kept working on my recovery. I finally got to one year of sobriety and then I continued to struggle for another year. I stopped making excuses, I recognized my defense mechanisms, I listened to others, I found my higher power, I worked on accepting that I am an alcoholic and drug addict and I focused on my recovery.

In recovery, I was able to identify and recognize the defense mechanisms of denial, blaming others for addiction, using humor to distance myself from my real problems, and numerous other defenses I used as a means of abstaining from treatment or contributing to relapses. I was also able to explore my faulty thinking that impacted my addiction and replace these negative thoughts with healthier thinking. I was prepared for the bad days and had a plan when every day in recovery did not go as I would have liked. Now, I find amazing things in recovery. Aspects of my life changed for the better and I am extremely grateful. I went back to school and achieved my doctorate degree. I have a job I love and people in my life who love, trust, support and have faith in me. Life did not get easier for me, I just learned how to manage. I found that being in recovery for alcoholism and drug addiction did not mean that I was weak, a failure, fuck up, or something to be ashamed of but was something I could be proud of, I was resilient, strong, and empowered.

Gifts of Recovery

I will be attending AA/NA meetings as well as therapy sessions for the rest of my life. The only difference between the start of my recovery and now is that my perception has taken a 180-degree turn. I no longer feel ashamed about being in recovery but feel resilient, strong, and empowered. The journey was not easy, but I would not trade it for anything, and that is something I never thought I would say or feel.

In recovery, I have had both my daughters, Morgan and Eva. They are my heart. My wife and I are going strong, still in love, and plan to celebrate many more years of marriage together. Words cannot express all the gifts that recovery has brought me. It is my hope that people reading this will see the strength that those who are working treatment managing an addiction and/or mental health concern. For those struggling with an addiction or mental health concern, please don't give up, keep going, and know that you are resilient, strong, and empowered. The times where you may not feel strong and resilient in treatment are the times that others see it in you. When you continue your treatment with negative thoughts such as, *It won't work, it's a waste of time, or I just can't do it*, you must continue to work at it.

I want to send my appreciation and thanks to the readers of my story. It is my hope that through stories like mine and others in this book, we can shed the stigma of addiction and change the negative perception that currently exists about being in recovery and treatment. One statement I often make is that I strongly believe everyone could benefit from therapy or supportive groups. It does not have to be a reaction to a negative situation or crisis in our lives, but more as a means of strengthening our mental health. If there is any ambivalence towards seeking treatment and trying it out, ask yourself why. You may be experiencing the fear of stigma. What would others think of me? Will they think something is wrong with me? What actually does happen with treatment and recovery, regardless of why you began, is that you find that you are resilient, strong, and empowered! Hopefully, with more people working on their mental health, stigma will break!

Reflective Questions

Is there something from this chapter that resonated with you? What changes do you believe would be positive in your life?

For professionals or therapist in training? Have you seen a therapist? If not, why? I am a firm believer that if you are practicing to help others you should experience therapy and the feeling of sitting in a waiting room waiting for your therapist.

Patrick McElwaine, PsyD

Dr. Patrick McElwaine is an assistant professor of counseling psychology at Holy Family University and a faculty member at the Beck Institute. He has over twenty years clinical experience in various settings. Dr. McElwaine is a member of multiple professional psychology organizations and he serves on the Montgomery County Drug and Alcohol Advisory Council. At settings including the National Alliance on Mental Illness (NAMI), various school and hospital organizations, Pennsylvania Psychological Association (PPA) and the Lilly Conference, he has conducted numerous presentations related to mental health, addiction, stigma, and pedagogy.

In his free time, Dr McElwaine loves spending time with his wife and two daughters. He enjoys running and is an avid sports fan and a diehard Eagles fan.

CHAPTER SIX:
My Tapestry

Veronica Singleton, M.Ed., LPCA

Sharing one's personal story is rarely easy or simple, especially when doing so leaves you exposed, vulnerable, and risks destroying relationships that have taken decades to repair. My hope is that as you read my story you will understand that these are my perceptions of events. It is not my intention to denigrate anyone who may view things differently, rather it is to instill hope in those who can relate to my perceptions of these experiences.

While growing up, it was evident that there were glaring disparities between my family and others in our circle. My father, who I now believe did so to avoid dealing with my mother, worked extensive hours. Often out of town, he created reasons to stay away for as long as possible. My mother, well, she was an alcoholic. She relied on 'uppers' to get moving and 'downers' to relax. Her addictions created chaos. Abuse, neglect, and desperate parenting made up my childhood years.

At the age of four, I found often myself parenting my newborn sister. Endless hours would seemingly pass while I wallowed in my anxiety, afraid some harm would befall this precious infant and I would be to blame. What if I dropped her, or stuck her with a diaper pin, or burned her while feeding her a bottle? I got lucky, none of these things came to pass.

Eventually, I was off to school. Caring for her was no longer my problem, or so I thought. The distance between home and school should have afforded me a chance to take a break, to be a kid. Nope. Irrational, compulsive thoughts related to her well-being filled my overactive imagination, detracting from my ability to find peace throughout elementary school.

This did not change once she entered school. Once, while gazing out a classroom window, watching some students playing softball for gym class, I searched for her. Needing to see her, to know she was okay. I scanned the field, desperately trying to recall what she was wearing that day only to witness a student fall to the ground as a baseball bat unexpectedly and connected with their head. Through the open window, the vociferous *thunk* as bat and skull connect resounded.

My heart sank, my thoughts raced. *Do not let that be her*, I silently pled. Moments later, confirmation, I was called to the nurse's office to aid my sister. Helpless, my heart ached, for her and much more. The event brought me to a clear understanding of the parent-child bond. I had intensely experienced how deeply parents are supposed to *want to* love, care for and protect their children. To attend to us, rather than selfishly seek to be the 'cool' parents on the block. I sobbed.

In their infinite wisdom, my parents would throw parties on weekends for neighborhood teens and young adults. Free-flowing alcohol and live bands were ever-present in our basement. This, coupled with early puberty, confounded childhood leaving me in a constant state of insecurity and self-doubt as to my role in a world where I did not belong.

I know my parents loved us. The passage of time encouraged me to intellectualize that given their age, immaturity, and inexperience, they did the best they could. As an adult, I can relate. Countless times I have paused to wonder who thought I was capable and competent enough to make adult decisions. The intellectual rationalizations of my adulthood came much too late to have protected me from my childhood.

Having become parentified at such a young age, I rapidly became the 'mama' to all my friends, they confided in me and sought out tidbits of wisdom and advice when they felt they had nowhere else to turn. One night during a sleepover with one such friend, she disclosed her deepest darkest secret to me. This is when my world shattered. All remaining remnants of youthful optimism and hope were lost. Daddies do not do such things to their little girls. Do they?

I reported this to a trusted teacher, my mentor, and within days my friend disappeared. They packed up and ran and I never heard from her again. I vaguely remember a face to face interview, with some authority, but mostly what I remember is feeling numb. That numbness lasted for years.

As a result of my demolished naivety, I never looked at *my daddy* the same again, despite *his* lack of wrongdoing. I cannot explain why this was. I simply could not trust him, or any father figure in my life. My involuntary distrust was exacerbated by the confessions of other friends in the years that followed. My perspective became jaded, bitter and I found myself lacking the emotional intelligence and self-regulation to effectively manage my distress.

Late in my eleventh-year, defiance, and deviance took hold. I smoked a pack of cigarettes a day, disappeared for hours on end, and began drinking. Anything to escape the painful thoughts of home and returning there at the end of the day. Existential guilt arose in my mother and she sought help from a psychologist, who slapped a label of manic depressive on my forehead and sent us out the door. One visit was enough, treatment was unnecessary, she had been exonerated. No fault lay within her, nothing changed.

Decades of poor choices, egocentric, self-harming behaviors and attention-seeking ensued. Abusive relationships were the norm, self-fulfilling prophecy at its best. Headed toward alcoholism myself, I lost all faith that one day I would find a 'normal' life. Unable to truly connect with others and desperate for change all felt lost.

Enter my husband. He is a genuine, caring, affectionate, person. I should have felt like the luckiest woman on the planet, right? Not so fast. In my tangled web of irrational thinking, we had a problem. He was too good to be true.

You see, he walked into my life when I was one relationship removed from a long-lasting encounter with domestic violence. Searching desperately for a place to belong. A place where I could be me, whoever that was, without fear of judgement. I waited for the fallout so Armageddon could commence, and I could get on with my miserable existence, alone.

He truly believed in me and fought for us; others would have given up. Many times, as I stagnated in my mental illness, I tried to push him away. I even succeeded briefly a couple of times, for a moment or two. His steadfast resolve chipped away at my angst, piece by piece, slowly aiding in uncovering what he had always known was underneath the tough outer layer. An empathetic, caring soul in pain, vulnerable and seemingly alone. A woman who needed to heal.

His unwavering patience and love guided me from the darkness into a place where positivity blossomed to choke out the weeds that were so deeply rooted in my soul. He encouraged me to become the best me I could be, to never give up, to always strive to be a better version of me than I was yesterday. He tells me I have far exceeded his expectations, most days I believe him. It is harder now not to.

All these years later, he continues to tell me every day that I am beautiful. Most importantly, he provides an unending message that I am *enough* today, tomorrow and always. With a boundless, continued forward momentum, I press on. Not because I am obligated to do so, rather due to what my husband opened my eyes to, a simple, basic truth; I am not broken, I never was.

Together, we have raised four children, two girls, and two boys. Our eldest daughter does not share DNA with my husband. Still, he loves her as his own, demonstrating that same unconditional love, patience, and equality for her despite the lack of a genetic connection. Modeling skills I lacked, he strengthened my ability to effectively parent and actively love our children, even in the most difficult moments.

Our boys are on the autism spectrum, so ever-present in life was an abundance of counselors combating the myriad of challenges we faced. My demons included. Counselors who believed in me, in us, when I could not, saw potential, where I found none. Opened doors, when I had no key. Walking beside me, as I now do for others. I recognized as I emerged into the field of counseling, it is they who have aided me to find catharsis and have shown me the way home.

Becoming a counselor is not something I actively sought out. Instead, the counseling profession found me. Admittedly, in the dark recesses of my mind, when I dared to dream, there was an inherent love of others. A strong desire to make a difference for others having suffered through life in hopeless despair. As if on cue, in my thirty-sixth year, my daughter would forever change my life's trajectory for the better.

As is the case for many, I found myself fueled by a deep desire that my children rise above and surpass their parents in life. One of the messages frequently imparted upon our children became, "You are going to college after high school, even if I have to enroll with you to get you there." I never dreamed that the interpretation of this would be anything other than "college is important," yet my daughter heard and held closely to something different.

In 2007, she and I arrived at the local community college to enroll her for the fall semester. Forms completed, her course schedule in hand, she beamed at me with pride and uttered the most terrifying sentence I could imagine. "Your turn." Baffled, I merely looked at her while I struggled to comprehend her meaning.

"You promised me you would enroll with me," she stated matter of factly. The lightbulb went off with a thousand glaring watts staring me in the face.

"No, honey. That was a threat," I casually retorted.

"Well, I took it as a promise that you were doing this with me and if you don't go, I don't go."

Ninety minutes later, I had taken three computerized assessments, completed a college application, applied for financial aid, registered for the same general education classes as my daughter and left with a pile of textbooks. As the shock wore off, the realization set in. Not only was I old enough to have a college-aged daughter but I unexpectedly became a college student. Stop this ride! I want to get off, please.

Fortunately, even if I did not see it at the time, there was no stopping the ride.

When I look back through the timeline that has been my life, I am continually amazed at how each piece fits together and forms a seamless masterpiece. Each moment of misery, joy, pain, hope, fear, anxiety, hopelessness, helplessness, and despair woven together into an intricate tapestry, bound around the edges by people who believed in me Those who have come and gone, those who are still with me cheering me on as I go, still adding to and reinforcing the design. Most importantly, bringing to life the understanding of why I should believe in myself, reminding me I am who I am because of the relationships and experiences I have lived.

Every experience, good and bad further enhancing the story of my life. Every hobby, interest, fleeting adventure led me to the counseling profession. Yes, there were long, treacherous, winding roads along the way but there were beautiful scenic views providing just enough hope, strength and courage to keep traveling ahead.

Twelve years later I have completed not only a four-year degree but also a master's degree in counseling and human development. Oh, and I am halfway through a doctoral program in counselor education and supervision. All because my stubborn and amazingly wonderful daughter misconstrued the meaning and intention of something she had been told her entire life. I cannot thank her enough for motivating me to reach for the stars.

My story is only unique in so much as it is *my* lived experience. So many of us have traumatic histories to overcome, many far worse than my own. If I have learned anything from the painful experiences of my past, it is that there is nothing I would change. I hold strongly to this tenet, for if I were to change anything it would change everything, and I love who I have become.

Do not misunderstand me, I am still healing. There is always room for growth, but I have learned to love who I am today and who I will be tomorrow. For me, this came from uncovering the ability to accept what is and to look beyond one's self to understand the journey of others in relation to my own.

It is my hope that you will do the same. That you will find the courage to accept and overcome what is. That you see you already have the strength to love yourself, now in this very moment and in all the moments yet to come. Most importantly, I hope you find the wisdom to know that you are enough and to see that you are not broken, you never were.

From the Inside Out

Veronica Singleton, M.Ed., LPCA

Veronica resides in Kentucky with her husband of twenty-seven years and their four children. Her first grandchild was born in October of 2018. Her interests include teaching, research, gardening, crafting, traveling, reading and playing video and board games.

She currently works as a mental health counselor in a private practice and is an adjunct faculty member for a local college. She is a strong advocate for social justice, academic integrity, reducing stigma related to mental illness and addressing disparities in all underserved populations in the field of mental health.

She is an active member of the American Counseling Association and the Association for Counselor Educators and the Kentucky Counseling Association. Furthermore. She is conference committee chair for the Kentucky Mental Health Counselor Association, president of Upper Cumberland Division of Kentucky Mental Health Counselors Association, president of the Alpha Chi Omega chapter of Chi Sigma Iota, and secretary for the Kentucky Association for Gay, Lesbian, Bisexual and Transgender Issues in Counseling. She is pursuing her PhD in Counselor Education and Supervision.

CHAPTER SEVEN:

Between Two Worlds

Chun-Shin Taylor, Ph.D., LCPC

I first came to America in 1999 with the belief that if I just studied and worked hard, I would be successful. After all, I had complete faith that God directed me to this country. I felt that the American dream was within reach, but I quickly discovered myself falling into a deep hole within months. I felt torn between two worlds: the majority, and minority.

Within this hole, I fought with unbearable loneliness, unpredictable panic attacks, and unresolvable confusion. These things were combined with the stress from non-stop studying, lack of sleep, limited financial resources, navigating the language barrier, and culture shock increased my panic attacks and brought temporary vision loss. In those early months and years in this country, I felt as though I would die if I continued to stay, but knew going back home was not an option for fear of returning to Korea as a failure. I was terrified of proving my naysayers right when they told me how foolish my endeavor to America was. In this way, I felt stuck between two worlds again: Korea and America. It made me question my decision to come, though I knew I wanted to help couples and families through the counseling profession. Mostly, I started to question whether it was my will or God's will for me to be in this country. I was devastated.

During my studies, I met and married my Korean/Caucasian husband and, just like my journey to America, marriage proved to be much harder than I thought it would be. The more I tried to hold onto the marriage, the more I felt lost and alone. I did not feel as though I belonged in his community or my own. The messages each sent about my marriage were in direct conflict with one another: his family and community urged me to leave my marriage for my own happiness, whereas my side encouraged me to endure the relationship for the sake of our children. I felt torn and stuck between two worlds again. When I thought I was moving upwards, I only fell deeper into the hole. My family wanted me to return to Korea to start a new life, but I feared I could not live with the shame I knew my divorce would bring to my family. While visiting Korea, other family questioned why I traveled home without my husband, our children without their father, and I saw the pain and agony in my mother's face as she stood frozen, unable to provide an honorable response. I felt frozen with her, unable to hide and with nowhere to go.

I felt I could not escape the shame my family felt, both in Korea and here in America. I visited my brother in Ohio after my divorce, and clearly remember his and his wife's reluctance and hesitancy when their Korean friends asked why I traveled alone without my husband. I stood frozen, again, without an acceptable response. I do not recall how we managed that situation, but I remember no one mentioned about my divorce. I knew I tried to protect my brother's family, especially him being a pastor and to guard the honor of our family, leaving me feeling hurt and ashamed.

Feeling isolated and ashamed, I decided to seek support outside of my family and ethnic group. At first, this was not an easy endeavor. I felt awkward and invisible. My interactions with other consisted of a case of mixed identities, as many confused me with one of their other Asian friends they met elsewhere. I often felt alone, sitting quietly, at conferences, work, and class though I was surrounded by people. Our language and culture differences made it difficult to engage in conversations that were more than surface deep. I always felt that I was interrupting a group of people when I approached them for conversation, as there was usually silence for my efforts. Eventually, I formed deep and abiding friendships with people who did not judge me for my immigration or marital status. Instead, they became a trusted barometer to bounce my thoughts and emotional distress off without leaving me feeling judged and ashamed. They became the stepping-stones I needed to climb out of the hole of isolation and loneliness.

My American dream had always been to become a therapist, helping distressed couples and families. I felt it was my calling, but I struggled with navigating the career labyrinth as well as my own critical voice. I was a divorced and single mother of three within the Korean-American community. How could I realize my dream of helping couples and families when I couldn't even save my own marriage? At least, I hoped my secure legal status guaranteed my job because I learned from other immigrants how stressful and threatening life in America is until legal status is secured. After an exhausting search for a counselor position, my friend explained that it wasn't until she changed her Korean name to an American name, did she get callbacks for interviews and become hired in her field. But I could not give up my Korean name, which implies my father's hope for me. Because my last name changed when I became married, I felt an even stronger sense to keep my first name as a way to stay connected to my family and culture in Korea. Instead, I changed my job search strategy.

I lowered my expectations by searching for entry-level counselor positions only requiring a high school diploma. During my interview, my supervisor asked me why I applied for a position requiring a high school diploma when I had a master's degree. What a dreadful question that was! What I couldn't reveal in my response was the inner turmoil I faced during my job search because of my name, language proficiency, and fear. In part, I was afraid to find out how I would perform, compete, and survive in

America compared to other applicants. I did not allow these answers to escape my throat because I knew I needed to start somewhere and provide for my family. So, what I said instead was that I was interested in learning about American culture in our field and wanted to start from the bottom as I earned my licensure hours. This seemed an acceptable response, and so I landed my first job as a rehabilitation counselor.

It took another four years to achieve full licensure. At first, I felt like I had finally climbed out of the hole I was in, but then I quickly slipped back through. The language barrier became a critical issue because I felt limited in expressing myself in therapy sessions. Many of my colleagues and American friends said I spoke "excellent" English. Yet, I was left feeling unsure and confused by their platitudes as the world outside of my circle of friends and profession was much harsher and more critical toward me. Meanwhile, conducting therapy sessions with Korean clients was unexpectedly challenging because I was not familiar with certain therapeutic concepts and interventions in Korean. I was afraid to be judged as inadequate by both non-Korean and Korean clients. Moreover, I overly pressured myself to 'heal' my clients' wounds. Their stories were extremely important for them and for me; I could not afford to misunderstand anything. I started to feel burnt out. Rationally, I knew I was not completely responsible for my clients' healing, but emotionally, I felt like I was. I felt stuck between two worlds again.

By this time, my divorce was finalized, and I needed a breakthrough. I returned to school to pursue a doctorate degree. Emotionally, I felt completely burnt out and drained every day, and could barely manage to pull myself out of bed. Physically, I had to maintain daily life as a single mother. I had to go to work, attend classes, and take care of my three children who were about eleven, five, and two years old at the time. Financially, I was stressed and uncertain of how I would support us. There was a several-month gap while we waited for child support to be set, and I was looking for a full-time job. My experience growing up in a household of a poor, hardworking Korean family of nine helped prepare me for the pressure of living with so little. Even as a young person I had difficulty accepting help from others. I developed an outer sense of pride and self-sufficiency as a way to mask the inadequacy I felt on the inside. But as a mother, I had to learn to reach out to get help financially and emotionally, so that I could supply my children with their basic needs. I applied for the public assistance program. I vividly remember the first time I had to use my food stamp card. As I stood frozen in front of the cashier, my hands shook, and my mind went blank. I was overwhelmed with feelings of embarrassment, guilt, and shame as they felt like waves of a tsunami crashing over me. How did I get here? What did I do wrong? What happened to me? I was not prepared to experience such fear and vulnerability in the middle of a grocery store checkout line. I needed something more than public assistance and another degree to help keep me from experiencing the fear I felt that day.

Throughout this journey, I wrestled with God for purpose and meaning to my existence in this country. I continuously poured out my anger, disappointment, and hurt to Him as I felt it was my calling to travel across the Pacific Ocean. I left my family behind and endured seemingly unjustifiable and unjust events. It was the unanswered questions about these events that haunted me. The more I felt dragged down by them, the more I clung to God. I knew that He had a plan and purpose for me, I just couldn't see it at the time. Then, after spending twenty years in America struggling between two cultures, I began to realize God's plan and purpose for my life and this journey. My hope to comfort others who are in any affliction with the comfort that God has shown me (2 Corinthians 1:3-4) was what brought me to America. Distressed couples were in my mind when I left Korea even though I was not married and only saw distressed couples. But today, I know that the couples I desire the most to serve are interracial and interfaith couples and their children. I fully understand how complex it is to live in between two cultures, and how hard it is to create a shared place for interracial couples and their children. These same struggles are shared among immigrants of other cultures who come here to find themselves falling into a hole of culture shock and reconciling their own integration of faith, and their other culture.

Throughout my journey, I realized that God calls me as a 'partner in comfort' (2 Corinthians 1:7). Comfort does not mean comfortable, and comfort grounds in feelings of solidarity. Comfort comes from mutual partnership. I'm still in the process of learning to *suffer with* my clients, my wounded self, and my children. I believe that continued self-reflection in order to fight against our critical inner voice, harsh environment from living as a minority, and emotional injuries that were carried from our home cultures and families is a must. In doing so, a window of tolerance to cope with ambiguity and the unknown would expand. Unjustifiable events might continue, but I won't respond the same way as before. A burgeoning sense of anger and hurt would transform into courage that foster fight for the weak, the hurt, and the unseen. I learned that I could not do this alone. Reaching out to create and foster a supportive community with others became a necessary path to follow. Ultimately, I learned that I could fall into a hole again, but I know that I could come out stronger, healthier, and more balanced with help from myself, others, and God.

If you feel like you are stuck, in a deep hole, and uncertain about your direction in life, reach out for help, either to your friend, a parent, a religious leader, or a professional counselor. Learn to be courageous and vulnerable at the same time. In order to do so, please learn to discern between safe and unsafe people. Moreover, learn to become a safe person to yourself first. Learn to tolerate ambiguity over the nature of life and the purpose of your life. Learn to consider your suffering as a life-long sojourner whom you do not know well yet. Develop a relationship with suffering by learning to suffer with another human being who will teach you the joy of being there for someone in return.

Co-authored and Compiled by Jacqueline Rech

Chun-Shin Taylor, Ph.D., LCPC

Chun-Shin Taylor has served her clients and community as a clinical counselor, researcher, counseling educator, columnist, and clinical supervisor for the past fourteen years. She is an expert on Asian-American counseling, Asian-mixed race marriage, inter-generational conflicts, integration of religion/spirituality and counseling, relational and community trauma. Her passion is to bridge the gap between counseling research and clinical implication, especially in regard to stigma toward mental health, racial issues, and interfaith issues within Asian communities.

When she isn't sitting by a river with a good book, you can find Chun-Shin enjoying time with her three children, and their guinea pig, Butter.

Please visit her website at
www.livingharmonycounseling.com

CHAPTER EIGHT:
Perfectly Imperfect

Tammy Rovane, LMFT

"I'm perfect in my imperfections, happy in my pain, strong in my weakness and beautiful in my own way because I'm me."
~Unknown [2]

You will not be reading a story about how a *Leave It to Beaver* family went rogue. My story and family history consists, instead, of generations of trauma, substance abuse, crime, and poverty.

Although my life began in the ghettos of Sacramento, I was a statistic of poverty, trauma and lack or resources. The adults in my family were irresponsible; add their own struggles with addiction and trauma, and their ability to hold down a job was, for the most part, nonexistent. My family was poor, unstable, and very unpredictable. They often struggled to feed us and keep a roof over our heads. Their issues with drugs and crime were made worse by their sense of entitlement, which was unhealthy, to say the least on their best days. With caretakers unable to take care for their basic needs, it stands to reason I would become a victim of my environment. Though the odds were stacked against me, I chose not to continue my family's generational cycle of brokenness and abuse. And it would be years filled with more trauma before I was able to accept my perfect imperfections.

My Early Years

One of my first memories was missing my mom. No one could explain to me her frequent absences. During this time, she was gone for months. My sister's dad, who had no legal need to care for me (he was not married to our mother) was bitter at having to care for me while my mom was not around. I was a burden to him. His disdain was reflected in the way he spoke and treated me as compared to my sister, and on at least one occasion while playing outside unattended I was hit by a car. Not long after this a man— my biological father—was at our door with the police to take me away and drive me to Mississippi. If I thought he would provide the care and stability I needed, I was wrong. My time with him was marked by repeated abuse, as one of my first memories was of him teaching me how to "kiss real boys." I can still hear the opening of *Mork and Mindy* and picture the Jeep as I tried hard to focus on anything other than what was happening. I was a five-year-old lonely, lost, and confused girl who missed her mom.

When I was finally sent back home to be with my mom, I was hopeful that everything was going to be 'okay'. But it was not long before I realized the situation I left hadn't really changed. Corporal punishment was a frequent occurrence. My stepdad was easily frustrated by us and often joked about how to make the 'paddle' hurt more. My mom recalls coming home to find my lip busted on more than one occasion, but not once did she accept responsibility for her part in leaving us in his care. Even worse, I was molested for years by his nephew. I finally stood up to the nephew by threatening to reveal his abuse if he touched me again. He stopped, but the chaos around me would continue. My mom and stepdad seemed too busy getting high and partying. It was not unheard of to get the youngest "stoned" and use them for entertainment. Of course, when this was not happening adults were verbally and physically fighting on a regular basis. Did I mention there was unpredictable chaos on a regular basis?

One day in elementary school, my sister and I had walked home and arrived at a house that looked burglarized. We went to the neighbor's (who was an officer) and found out our mom had tried to commit suicide and the paramedics had to break out the windows to get to her. No one remembered my sister and me.

The violence only grew worse. Doors were kicked in, furniture tossed, tires punctured, and cars were keyed. I don't think anyone thought about how any of this was affecting us. During my eighth-grade year my family's toxic belief that "any drugs were better than drinking" (my mom's parents were alcoholics and my stepdad was one as well). My mom felt that drinking ruined a family more than any other substance could. This led to a family member pushing meth on me at the age of thirteen. I felt trapped, unable to make sense of it all. I hope I've given you a sense for the chaos in my life. It would prove to be a tragic mistake as meth would shatter my cousins and sibling.

Getting Out

Growing up in such an unhealthy environment made me feel like the odd one out of any social group. I didn't fit in with kids at school because my parents did not allow me to participate in any activity that required any of their participation. Then, as if life was not traumatic enough, I had issues enrolling in high school because my mom had been enrolling me in school by my stepdad's last name, instead of my legal name. I didn't even know my own legal name! But from that point on, I was able to go through life as Tammy Wolff, my true legal and birth name.

It was shortly after I turned fourteen that I started working to make my own money with the goal of being able to escape my family and have a better life for myself. The more effort I made to improve my life, the more my family tried to bring me down by making fun of me for being "stuck up" and not living their lifestyle. While working at my first job I would meet the person that would change my trajectory and have the most effect on my short fourteen-year-old life. Sheryl became a close mentor and friend. She had taken me home one night after my family had "forgotten" to pick me up. That night was the start of our friendship. She showed me what a healthy teenager looks like. When I was sixteen, she received a promotion in Fresno for work. She asked me to go with her. This was my chance to escape, so I left. She acted as my guardian and enrolled me in school. I not only fit in time to work hard on homework, but also two jobs to help pay the bills. She taught me what it takes to be a hard worker and a good person.

Sheryl and I moved back to Sacramento after two years and continued to be roommates. One day we had gone to the State Fair with her sister and a couple of their friends. Her sister didn't like who her husband's friend was dating and joked about someone, anyone, to date him instead. Everyone who knew this man's reputation passed on the opportunity, but I didn't know. I was excited to date him.

Finding Me

He was great. Until he wasn't. He treated me poorly in the beginning by pushing me away and then pulling me back, and yet I kept going back. I should have realized then that he wasn't healthy or good for me. But with so many mixed messages about love from my upbringing, how could I separate the good and bad of this relationship? I fell hard for him and we ended up getting married. Our marriage was a struggle, especially at the beginning as most marriages are. I feel that ours was complicated by my trust issues, but eventually, he became my best friend. I confided in him and turned to him for everything. We grounded each other, and he was excited for me to go back to school. He had said he looked forward to taking care of our boys so we could give our boys, as well as ourselves, a wonderful life.

My classes were demanding, and I missed my family while at school. But I felt this arrangement was going to give my boys the best balance of time with their dad and with me. I was also excited about therapy I had to do for grad school, and could use therapy for hours towards my MFT license. I used my time in therapy to understand and meet my needs within my marriage, work, and friendships. In hindsight, this experience in grad school only highlighted the need for continued personal therapy while in my career. But unfortunately, I didn't quite understand the importance then and didn't continue therapy. I incorrectly thought I was fine without it and discovered that I had no internal resources or reserves for any crisis.

At the end of 2007, I was diagnosed with Chiari Malformation and within three months was having a decompression brain surgery. I had several complications and was in and out of ICU four or five times with three or four surgeries and ended up with a VP shunt by the end of 2008. It was horrible to be that sick. I shudder to think how scary it was for my boys, who were in seventh, fourth, and second grades, to see me like that.

While I was still recovering in the spring of 2009, I went to work as usual. While reviewing an enormous cell phone bill, my world shattered. It revealed my husband's hidden affair. The man who I had considered to be my best friend never spoke to me again after my discovery. When I realized how much he protected his mistress, it made me realize the lengths he would go to make me the 'bad guy' when clearly, I could do a fine job of that on my own. I always did my best to have integrity, though I struggled with showing grace. I tried not to collude with his gaslighting and just focused on co-parenting. But he never encouraged the boys to recognize my role in their lives. He simply acted as if I did not exist. His outright refusal to co-parent our children was maddening, and I did not react well. I have since had to process through my behavior with my boys. The therapy I had during my program at school was not sufficient enough to hold me up through this dark time in my life.

I internalized my husband's affair, believing I wasn't good enough. The loss of the marriage triggered childhood trauma, and flashbacks. It was a difficult road to travel alone, so I reentered therapy. As a single mom, and full-time employee I was depressed at having no family resources. I had to constantly remind myself that sometimes things have to get worse before they can get better, but even so, no one wanted to be around me. Hell, I didn't want to be around me. I felt broken and unworthy of anyone's love and care, which only served to push all my closest friends away. Through therapy, I was able to learn how to become a better mom, while processing through the damage my own family, and husband's infidelity caused. I wanted to provide a life in which my boys could be kids and have fun without repeating unhealthy cycles, and I succeeded. It was not easy, and I am not perfect, but I am definitely good enough. How I managed to escape, and break that cycle is amazing.

When I look at that time in my life the most upsetting thing for me is that my three boys witnessed all that chaos. Although I could not prevent my boys from suffering through the divorce process, I could at least take control of my own healing. I was motivated by my love for my boys to develop the resilience I needed to continue this journey, and found the courage to take ownership for my part in their suffering. It was traumatic and upsetting for me to see them suffer through their abandonment issues, as they were unwilling victims of our adult decisions. I began by regaining my power and faced all the ways I played into other people's versions of me. It would be the start of my journey of personal growth. Because I had some of the skills from therapy earlier in my life and actually being a therapist, I knew where to start. I needed to find a therapist. I had a friend at work recommend a therapist and I started seeing her weekly. It is important to note that just because I am a therapist does not mean that I am able to help myself in the insightful ways I can my clients. With that said, neither does it mean I am in any way a 'bad' therapist. It means I am human. So, when I realized that I was letting others chose who I was and what my needs "should' be I knew that I needed to change that. My with poor sense of self, especially after years of letting my ex-husband bully and gaslight me, I had no clue who 'me' was and was second-guessing myself all the time. I did not know exactly how, but I knew I could and had to change my life. It was the hardest this to do. Therapy is not easy. Going through the toughest times in life will be gut-wrenching, but worth it in the grand scheme of life. To learn so much about yourself and to learn how to love and be kind to yourself is by far the greatest gift you can ever give someone let alone yourself. To be able to feel and live your authentic life and be at peace with it, even though you know its flawed is empowering and freeing. Therapy has done that for me.

    I did not have the resilience or skills at the beginning of the divorce and because of that I was not able to avoid creating or to help or prevent some of the conflict, in turn, my boys didn't get the mom they deserved. This experience has fueled my passion as a therapist for helping individuals find their inner strength, and purpose for their lives, and to learn how to better trust their own instincts rather than seek approval from others. I want to teach resilience to my clients, and the ability to show compassion toward others. Seeing my clients grow in confidence as they develop strength of character is an amazing feeling as a therapist.

While people who have experienced trauma or abuse are left feeling broken or misunderstood, they also often feel as if no one will accept them, or stay long enough to love them. It may be hard to imagine living life never hearing encouragements like, "I am proud of you," "you are so smart," "you can do anything you set your mind to," but for many with similar upbringings, this is their reality. Some feel that just knowing how they'd like to feel or behave is enough to make changes. Human behavior, however, is more complicated than that. It takes time for these individuals to learn the coping skills, emotional intelligence, and self-awareness it takes to begin implementing positive change. My hope for someone reading this is that you're able to embrace life as a journey of perpetual growth and knowledge. While we may have had very little control over the events that got us to this point in our lives, it is certainly now up to us to find a path of healing that feels authentic. We all have done the best we can, especially in these types of circumstances, and the way we cope while experiencing trauma has helped us to survive. But as we grow and no longer find ourselves in the same situations, these ways of coping become maladaptive behaviors and are no longer needed. Our society would be more effective at helping heal those who suffer by extending them compassion and care, instead of judgement, as we learn to change our maladaptive behaviors. Remember, we are all *perfectly imperfect*.

Teaching self-compassion while providing a non-judgmental atmosphere is a passion of mine. As a therapist I have gravitated towards working with adults especially individuals who struggle with borderline personality disorder, complex trauma, and dissociative disorders. I never imagined my past trauma could pave the road for me to provide hope for so many people throughout my career. I want to show people how to believe in themselves, not collude with others, manage the stresses of life, and process their pasts in healthy ways. I want to show others that there is no perfect way to heal, and that making mistakes along the way is a necessary step towards reaching their destination. Lastly, I want to provide a safe space for my clients to feel validated in their grief, or whatever it is they have been through, so they can be open to learning healthier coping and social skills while being able to embrace self-love and self-care We all have the ability to learn new skills and access resources to make positive changes. I am honored at this point in my own healing journey and career to nurture another's own growth and healing process as they embrace their perfect imperfections.

Tammy Rovane, LMFT

Tammy Rovane is from Sacramento, CA, where she's a licensed marriage and family therapist (LMFT) and proud mom of three amazing boys. Tammy's passion is to help bring awareness to mental health issues, specifically those related to complex trauma which spurred her desire to specialize in dialectical behavioral therapy (DBT) and her focus on working with adults with childhood trauma as well as individuals with borderline personality disorder.

When Tammy is not working as a therapist, she spends time with her boys and four-legged fur babies. She loves reading as well as traveling and relaxing with her husband and girlfriends.

CHAPTER NINE:
Bitter or Better

Danielle Proch-Vonbartheld, LMHC, NCC

My life has been a roller coaster for as far back as I can remember. My parents divorced in the 1970's when divorce was still taboo by society's standards. There was not a lot of stability in my life since both parents were still trying to figure out how to 'do life' and find happiness as they dated other people. During this time in my life, I witnessed domestic violence and mental illness. The underlying message that I sensed from family and friends was something was wrong with us. I felt that we were being judged and looked down upon with pity because of our broken home. I interpreted that to mean that something was wrong with me. I felt as if I was not loveable, and unworthy of love.

At the age of twenty, I was a full-time college student and working full-time as a retail manager. I fell in love and got married for the first time. I gave up college and had my daughter within the first two years of being married. My marriage did not go well. We didn't know how to relate to each other in healthy ways. Not long after our daughter was born, we divorced. I moved to Pennsylvania to be near my mom and maternal grandparents to have family support. I felt like something was wrong with me because 'I failed'. I didn't finish school and I failed at marriage. The same feelings permeated my life of not being good enough, worthy or lovable.

After moving to Pennsylvania, I met my second husband and we married in a Catholic church. I was very scared to get married a second time due to my previous failed marriage. Despite my fears, we married. In 2006, eleven years after being married for the second time, my life imploded. Those original feelings of being a failure, not worthy or lovable permeated my core. I felt as if I was midway through my life and I had not achieved my original dream of returning to college and pursuing a real career. The underlying feelings of not being worthy, being a failure and not being lovable had made me unhappy, angry and a negative person on the inside. I hid it well from most, but my unhappiness was projected onto my husband. He could not understand why I was so unhappy. We seemed to be living the American dream; we had it all. Our family consisted of 3 happy and well-behaved children. He had a great job, I worked full-time in retail we purchased a home and were 'living the dream'. I could not figure out why I could not find happiness. I didn't realize that the underlying feelings of being a failure were driving my unhappiness.

The constant thoughts of being a failure, worthless and unlovable propelled me to find an escape to my current reality. I blamed my husband for everything, and it showed. He was stressed trying to keep our family afloat while struggling to keep me happy at the same time. It all came to a head when he found out I was talking to someone online. I had been having an emotional affair and he was devastated. He loved me with all that he had and couldn't understand why his best to make me happy was not enough. He felt like he failed me, failed himself and our family. We both did not understand at the time that happiness comes from within. We weren't aware that we couldn't make each other happy. He couldn't make me happy; I was responsible for my own happiness. Sadly, my emotional affair was more than he could bear under the weight of his health and work stress as well as the pressures of daily life. He committed suicide on October 17, 2006. My life was changed forever. Those past feelings of not being loveable, worthlessness and that I was defective in some way were magnified by guilt, shame, judgment and yet another failure. It was almost too much for me to bear.

What saved me was an inexplicable inner feeling that God was with me. I feel that I have always had a gift from God of a grain of sand of hope in my life. I have always known that things would get better no matter how dark they looked. I felt that again during this time. My life would never look the same, there was much work to be done, but ultimately, I was going to be okay.

The questions in the aftermath of this tragedy became how am I going to handle this for my children; "Am I going to be bitter or am I going to be better?" Lao Tzu said, "The journey of a thousand miles begins with the first step." My healing journey began, and I eventually choose better. Choosing better was learning to allow myself to experience pain. I cried a lot, I yelled at times in my car, "Why me?" I was broken into tiny pieces. The weight of my shame and guilt were tremendous. Feeling these feelings felt like a heavy blanket was weighing me down and I felt as if I was never going to feel better. As the waves of grief crashed over me and pulled me under daily, I noticed that there were starting to be days when I didn't cry all day and that the storms of intense grief were slowly subsiding. I learned to feel *all* the losses and grieve all the past and current pain. The grieving process consisted of grieving the dreams of not having a 'normal' childhood, not finishing school, having a lasting marriage, a successful career and being loved in the way I needed to be loved while just being me. I was afraid to be vulnerable and that the real me was not good enough to be loved and accepted. I learned to look in the mirror at things I needed to work on, not turning to others to define my worth and took responsibility for my own happiness.

Over time, I learned that I had to set boundaries with others. I cut some people out of my life and learned to limit the amount of negativity in my life. I had to teach others how to treat me. I had to learn to communicate my feelings even when others won't like it or accept them. My worth is no longer based on others opinion. I had to learn that rejection does not define me. My life was broken like shattered glass and it was up to me to figure out how to piece it back together. Everywhere I turned I was being judged. There were not many supportive people in my life. Judgment kept me stuck in the guilt and shame. I took everything personally and was always on the defensive. I felt inadequate. I did not have enough acceptance and patience for myself or others. I had the weight of the world on my shoulders. My thoughts kept coming back to "what is wrong with me, why can't I just be happy".

The judgments of others weighed heavy on my heart. All my focus turned to my children as I sunk into an isolated, lonely existence. This tragedy made me realize I needed to make some drastic changes. I truly believe that hindsight is 20/20. Everyone says that, but until you live it, you don't really believe it to be true. When I look back over the last week that my husband was alive, I see all the signs that he was deeply depressed and in a mental health crisis. I was a retail manager, not aware of the warning signs of mental health. Looking back, he had been depressed for a long time and had no desire to address it with his doctor. Society deems that men are 'weak' if they seek assistance and that shame is very real. He refused to obtain help. I thought since HIPAA was the new buzz word at the time that I couldn't reach out to his doctor. The truth is, I could have provided the doctor with information; they just could not give me any.

My family members blamed me and asked how I could have done this to him. In the midst of anguish, I felt God with me. There is really no way to explain why I felt this way. Some people think you are crazy when you talk about it, but I was comforted in the knowledge that I believed everything was going to be okay. Even in the worst of times, I held a grain of sand of hope that things would eventually be okay. I was going to make it through this. I wasn't sure how or when, but I would be okay. God placed people in my path to help me redefine my spiritual beliefs. I always felt spiritual but suppressed this side of me. This was my opportunity to reconnect with God.

I am an introvert. I love being around others but need to be by myself to recharge my energy. I worked in retail and was involved in customer service so when I was not working, I liked to be home by myself or with my family. I was not much of a joiner. God had other plans, He kept putting a particular person in my path. She lived in my town and kept asking me to join her Bible study. She told me how uncomfortable she was asking me to join her women's bible study. She had never hosted one before, let alone invited a person she barely knew to attend it. She told me that God told her to ask me. I politely declined. God continued putting her in my path. I'd go to the grocery store and she was there. I'd go to the park and she was there. I went to a different park and she was there. It was getting creepy. I finally looked up at the sky and said, "Okay, God, I've got the message now." I joined her bible study of women and for the first six months I just sat in the bible study and cried. These women created the space for me to grieve and at the same time accepted me, broken and all. I had never met these women before, and they became my support system for the next three years.

I began counseling again. This time with a different counselor who helped me focus on the positive aspects of my life and not what I was lacking. Over time, I examined the people in my life one by one. I looked at their lives and levels of happiness and realized that they were not the experts in my life by any means. My judgment comes from God and God alone. I had to make God's word the foundation for my life. I believe that He is in control, He created me, and He does not make mistakes. I turned to the Bible to learn what God said about me. I found many scriptures that tell us what God thinks about His creations and his vast love for us. I wrote down these scriptures and carried them with me. They became my 'go-to' words of hope. When the negative feelings overwhelmed me, I needed to remember that "I am a child of the highest God. I am fearfully and wonderfully made. I am forgiven and I am loved". I had to learn to love myself. These words became the mantras to set the foundation of my inner peace.

I reexamined my life and reflected on some of the desires I had when I was younger. I wanted to become a writer. but this tragedy filled me with the desire to help others. I decided to go back to school and become a mental health counselor. The years in college with three children were hard. When I wasn't working, I was doing homework. During this time, I remarried, and my husband Chris became my biggest cheerleader. He encouraged me whenever I was ready to quit. Finally, in 2014, I earned my Master's in Arts in Professional Counseling degree from Liberty University. It was difficult finding an internship, but it turned into a bigger blessing than I imagined. It turned into a full-time job as a bereavement counselor and my dream had come true.

The pain and subsequent growth that I endured is what prepared me to sit in the counselor's seat. I feel that God dragged me, for years, through broken glass to smooth out my rough edges. I have been described in my youth as a diamond in the rough. The experience allowed me to learn the skills needed to walk alongside others in their pain. I am non-judgmental, patient and accepting of others no matter where they are in their journey. I've learned to speak the truth when I have to confront others, but it's wrapped with love. If I had not gone through that tragedy, I do not believe I would be an effective counselor. God showed up in my life and made good out of a really bad situation. I have learned to love and accept myself so that I can best love others.

In 2015, my family and I moved to Florida, where I am currently a licensed mental health counselor supervisor in a community mental health center. I love my job. Hopefully, I have played an important role in many individual's mental health journey. Looking back, it seems so obvious to me now that my late husband was in a mental health crisis. I have learned that we are all connected, and we need to be there for each other. Relationships are the most important things in this life, not possessions, accomplishments or vacations. At the end of our lives, no one has a U-Haul behind the hearse; we cannot take our stuff with us. I hope to continue to live with the end in mind, take no one for granted and offer others the best of me.

It is essential to continue to love and accept ourselves, mistakes and all, to be vulnerable, confront others with love, be present, and practice self-care so we can be our best selves for the people in our lives. Practicing positive inner self-encouragement using words such as " I have what others need; I am loved, and I am forgiven" can make all the difference in the way we treat ourselves and ultimately the way we treat others. The world needs more of our authentic selves. In the end, I hope you choose to be better instead of bitter.

Co-authored and Compiled by Jacqueline Rech

Danielle Proch-Vonbartheld, LMHC, NCC

Danielle returned to college in 2007 after a long career in retail management. Danielle graduated from Liberty University with a Bachelor of Science in Psychology: Christian Counseling in 2011 and also earned her Master of Arts in Professional Counseling there in 2014. She has experience working in various counseling settings including hospice, inpatient addiction treatment and currently provides therapy and supervision at a non-profit community behavioral health center and through her private e-counseling practice Inner Peace Counseling & Wellness, LLC as well as health coaching.

Danielle moved from Pennsylvania to sunny Florida in 2015 with her husband and two sons. She has a daughter, son-in-law and two beautiful granddaughters that she loves to visit back in PA. Her passion is to walk alongside others in their pain and guide them towards acceptance, forgiveness, and love. Danielle's hobbies include reading, writing, swimming, learning, walks on the beach and spending time with family and friends. Spirituality is important in Danielle's life and is the foundation that guides her to love others with the ongoing goal of loving others unconditionally.

CHAPTER TEN:

Blessed by the Broken Road

Kesha "The Confidence Converter" Jackson, LPC

My deepest desire is for my clients to understand that I am first and foremost a human, with insecurities, struggles, and heartache like them. My search for identity and self-confidence was a journey that began long ago. For as long as I can remember, my friends have come to me for advice on different aspects of their lives. I have always had the ability to come alongside them in a way that encouraged them to seek out their own conclusions and answers to whatever it was that bothered them.

During childhood, I struggled with finding my identity and self-esteem. I was the victim of bullying during a time when it was not as openly discussed as it is today. My family was considered poor, and though my confidence was already severely damaged, I had a few close friends in my neighborhood. Those friendships changed, however, when my sister developed a then undiagnosed mental health disorder.

The first time I realized something was different about her was when she stood up at a sleepover I was hosting and stated that she was someone called, "Stephanie Mills." At first, I thought she was playing but then several other personalities began to emerge during that sleepover. My sister became belligerent and my guests became frightened and requested to go home. I became the laughing-stock of our neighborhood, and my friends abruptly stopped coming over. My sister would go on to have many other episodes of what later was diagnosed as schizophrenia. No one in our family had ever been diagnosed with a mental health disorder, so it was uncommon. My mother believed that what happened in our house stayed in our house, so instead of getting help and taking my sister to a therapist she let it go. During my sister's episodes she would become another person and become involved in illegal and dangerous activities, among other things.

Our mother worked hard and was so focused on providing for my other siblings and me to notice my older sister's symptoms getting worse. Even if she had noticed, I don't think she really knew how to best respond. Many nights, I was the only one home to answer phone calls from the police officers who were trying to inform my mother of my sister's arrest. Due to my sister's volatile outbursts during her arrest, she was sent away to a mental health facility. My days were then spent visiting my sister after school. I noticed the other patients in the facility appeared like zombies, which both terrified me and caused me to feel great compassion toward them. I didn't feel as though they all needed to be so heavily medicated, and that some could really benefit from caring and compassionate treatment.

It was due to these many trips to visit my sister that I became fascinated with the human mind. I no longer felt like the girl who gave her friends advice, but instead could imagine myself delivering the kind of therapeutic interventions these patients needed. I fought my desire to become a therapist for years, I think as a way to distance myself from a childhood spent watching my sister's condition deteriorate. But during my last year of college, I decided to change my major from accounting to psychology. Again, I was fascinated with learning about the many treatment modalities and psychological philosophies used to assist clients through the challenges they faced. This change added a year to my undergraduate studies, but I did not care. I was focused on learning more about my sister's mental health and ways to help her and others struggling with similar conditions. This desire is what lead me to become a therapist.

Initially, we thought my sister's diagnosis could be hereditary, but it was later discovered that the onset of her symptoms was directly related to a bad batch of illicit substances laced with a dangerous hallucinogenic drug. From the moment the drug hit her bloodstream, she would never be the same, and neither would I. Her mental health and other behavioral and legal issues seemed to rise to the top of priorities for my mother.

In the wake of my sister's diagnosis, I was the one who became responsible for caring for the rest of our family. My mother considered me the "strong one," when in reality I felt like the bird with the broken wing. I craved the love and attention from my mother that I did not feel I received, and came to resent my sister for "stealing" my mother's time, attention, and love. Over the years, my resentments piled up as I became the standby caregiver for her children when she experienced her mental health symptoms. When my nephew passed away, it took me decades for me to find forgiveness for and resolve the issues with my mother, and sister. I also needed to forgive myself.

Today, my sister, mother, and I share a much better relationship. I am able to discuss the past with greater compassion and empathy, without placing blame. My sister has become stable through treatment, and continues to monitor her own progress. But despite all this now, I still struggled before I sought therapy for myself.

During the time when I still felt resentment towards my sister, and unloved or ignored by my mother, I met my first husband. I had just completed my bachelor's degree. I had moved to an unknown city with no friends or family and I was looking forward to earning my master's degree to fulfill my dream of becoming a therapist. I never imagined that my life with my ex-husband would spiral out of control like it did. While I was pursuing a degree towards becoming a therapist, it would be me that most needed the emotional life preserver and therapy to make sense of a lifetime of resentment and insecurities, in addition to the chaos that was about to become evident in my own personal life.

I didn't know it at the time we met, but my first husband suffered from multiple co-occurring issues pertaining to his own mental health and substance dependence. I didn't discover this until we were well into the relationship, but by then I felt trapped. As I look back now, there were several red flags that I either did not see or just ignored. I should have known about his struggles when he borrowed my car and disappeared for days, ignoring my calls and attempts to find him. I should have known there were deeper issues to discover when he constantly needed to borrow money without the ability to repay it, or when valuables went missing. But then I was not well informed about things like codependency or drug addiction from an adult perspective. I only had experience of watching my parents struggle with similar things in their marriage without fully understanding their implications.

Even though the red flags were there, I still dove deeper into the relationship rather than flee from it. I think in a way I felt that I could do better than my mother, and somehow this man would change for me; that his love for me would surpass his love for any substance. But after many years of reflection and time spent picking up the pieces in the aftermath, I realized my ex-husband came into my life while I was very vulnerable and seeking from him something he could not possibly provide. When we met, I already felt bitterness towards my family; I was searching for love from my childhood and I felt like damaged goods. Every relationship before his had ended in infidelity, abuse, or an inability to return my investment into the relationship.

I was in a position to be taken advantage of, and my ex-husband did just that. This caused a lot of stress at the beginning of our relationship. He continued to lie, steal, and cheat. Multiple cars of mine were sold to people to pay for his addiction throughout the course of our relationship. Throughout this time my ex proposed to me often, but I always refused. I knew that I shouldn't be involved with someone like him, but I didn't know how to get out of the mess I found myself in. I was in a downward spiral of codependency and went back and forth between feeling hope for the relationship, then despair and resentment. It was absolute chaos. My thoughts constantly turned back to the man I met before my ex-husband.

I met this other man just prior to his incarceration. What began as a friendship, soon blossomed into something more. We enjoyed each other's company, and our deep conversations covered every topic of life. They made me see myself in a better light and made me think I could continue to pursue my dreams. He was an over the road truck driver so we would talk often on the phone while he worked. The whole time I got to know him, I did not know about his legal issues or pending incarceration. After a few months, he asked me to be his woman and we decided to take our relationship in a different direction. But by the next day, he was gone. Disappeared! I couldn't reach him on the telephone or find him. I waited for his calls for months, but they never came. I assumed that he dropped our relationship and didn't know how to tell me.

Months went by, and that's when I met my ex-husband. One day I got a call from this other man, John, explaining that he had been incarcerated. I was already deeply involved with my ex, and explained this to John. He explained that when he met me, he was focused on enjoying our time together, so he didn't know how to explain his legal issues or pending incarceration. He wrote me love letters and called every day, and became a buffer to the chaos I was experiencing with my ex. I found myself struggling with two men: the first who poured out the care and affection I was looking for but was incarcerated without a release in sight, and the second who was there in person showing care, but also brought much stress and chaos to my life. Both men knew about the other. My ex wanted me to leave John alone, and although John wanted me to live my life even if it wasn't with him, he still knew I should not have stayed with my ex.

Eventually, the emotional struggles between loving a man I couldn't be with and not loving a man that I physically was with became too much. I was emotional and distracted all the time, and I ended up getting into a major car accident. I didn't know it at the time, but this accident would change everything. I almost lost my life in that accident, but instead suffered a concussion, cuts, bruises, and broken ribs. Though I was in great physical pain, the emotional pain of not having John there beside me was even greater. I wasn't able to care for myself, so my ex started caring for me. For a short time, he seemed to change his ways. I still questioned if I was staying in the relationship out of loneliness, or even a mental health condition I wasn't aware of, but he didn't stay out all night, and for my six-week recovery he would cook, and clean, and carry me so I could bathe. I finally saw in my ex what I was hoping to see all along: a man who finally cared for me and would take care of me. Suddenly, his bad qualities and chaos of the past year seemed to pale in comparison to this new man before me.

Instead of focusing on the love I still wasn't sure I felt for him, I focused on the love that he was able to give to me. So, even though there were still the red flags of addiction, and against many people's advice to end my relationship with him, I decided to accept his next proposal. Even though I knew I didn't love him enough to be in a marriage, and even though he went missing the night before our wedding, I still found myself standing at the altar saying, "I do." I wish I had listened to the voice that told me to turn around as I walked down the aisle, it would have saved so much more stress and chaos.

After we were married, I knew I had to write to John to let him know what happened and that I needed to focus on my marriage. I explained that he needed to end contact with me and continue with his life. Even though I knew I still loved John, I had just made a commitment to God and needed to uphold that vow.

John sent me a letter back and for the first time in our existence, I felt his anger when he said that I sat him to the side for a "fucking crack head" instead of waiting to see how much time he was facing. He told me he loved me, that I needed to do what was best for me and he would honor my request. I cried for days after reading his letter. I felt like I had lost the love of my life.

Right after the ceremony, my ex went right back to his old behaviors of leaving for days right after a payday, of losing employment, and stealing from my account. He began to use in our house, and I'd come home to find paraphernalia in the bathroom. I was thankful that my kids from a previous relationship did not see or find it. My relationship with my children began to suffer because, although I did not take drugs, I allowed a man who did to remain in our home. I was torn between being a good mother and being a good wife.

When my oldest son started to use substances, I felt like I had no grounds to set boundaries with him because of the chaos I allowed in our home. He was in conflict with my ex on many occasions, and life at home became a living hell.

My middle son hated my ex for everything he put me through, and so he ran away. I worried incessantly for his emotional well-being. He stayed at school more than home and his friends would relate the things he shared about our home life. My daughter kept to herself, usually in her room. She displayed behaviors consistent with her attempts at trying to deal with what was going on at home. I was completely embarrassed and felt helpless about how to help stop it all and help my children.

Despite the continuing chaos, I managed to make it to my last year of graduate school. My oldest two were graduating high school, and my youngest was entering the eighth grade.

That's when I discovered I was pregnant due to failed oral contraception while on a strong antibiotic. I made the physician take the pregnancy test three times. What the hell was I going to do with an infant when I had a drug-addicted husband? I thought it was all God's version of a sick joke. I had a moment where I thought I would end my pregnancy, but my ex convinced me otherwise. Looking back, I realize this was the best thing my ex did for me because I love my youngest son with all my heart.

Once I decided to continue with this last pregnancy, my ex began using more often. I needed a better life for the child I was carrying, so I filed for an annulment and my ex entered inpatient treatment. While in treatment, he begged me to try again and foolishly, I did. I was trapped by my own codependency. Unsurprisingly, nothing changed when he returned from treatment. If anything, things became worse. He resorted to threatening physical violence in order to get money from me, he would take from me while I slept, or defraud the bank deposit system. The mounting stress and financial instability put me in the hospital during my pregnancy for stress-related symptoms.

I hid my personal life well. No one at work had any idea what was happening at home. I dressed well and hid the pain behind a smile and clean pressed and stylish clothing, but underneath it all, I was falling apart. Without John there as a buffer from the chaos, I began having panic attacks. I knew that my mental health was in trouble.

Soon my youngest son would be born after a thirty-six-hour induced labor and subsequent C-section due to infant distress. When he stopped breathing after delivery, I had a full-blown panic attack. I had to be sedated while I was sutured, and the doctors had to administer oxygen because I stopped breathing.

While this was happening, my ex was selling my brand-new truck, my wedding rings, any other jewelry he could find, and taking money from my business account, and any money the kids had in the house.

When I was discharged the next day, he had no way to provide us a way home. My sister had to take us home and even though I needed to be on bed rest I had to go to the store to buy all the things my family would need during my recovery. I could not and did not trust my ex. I decided I had enough. I reached my breaking point.

When my new baby was a month old, I decided to go to therapy and seek mental health. In the beginning, during the first year, I went to a session every week. My therapist wanted to use medication management in addition to our sessions, but because I had a baby to care for at home, I did not feel that I could accept the medicine. I was diagnosed with adjustment disorder coupled with panic attack syndrome. I worked hard at my mental health recovery, and added books as a supplement to therapy. I read several self-help books which included: *The Seat of the Soul*, *Ayanla Vanzant*, and *The White Eagle* series. I also strengthened my relationship with God.

Eventually, I grew strong enough to face my demons. When my baby was six months old, I filed for divorce and made sure to follow through with it this time. I reduced my therapy to twice a month during the second year. During the third year, I reduced my therapy visits to every two months and then every six months just for maintenance.

While my life still comes with some challenges, I stay focused on the positive things and the many joys that come from surviving my life with my ex-husband. I realize while he was addicted to drugs I was addicted to chaos and had become co-dependent on him and his lifestyle. What was crazy had become my normal, despite knowing that it was not.

My baby, aka, "God's practical joke." is now thirteen years old. I am blessed to say that I have not had a panic attack in twelve years. I am a business owner, and licensed therapist. I am looking forward to retirement from my day job shortly to practice therapy on a full-time basis. I am also an author of children's books. I am a foster parent to several children in my area who have mental health challenges. I am a grandmother.

Today, I no longer physically go to therapy, however, as a requirement for my therapeutic license, I maintain a mentorship and supervision with other clinicians to keep me on track. I journal a great deal. I pay close attention to the warning signs of stress. I color and listen to music when I think that life is becoming stressful. I go get a weekly body massage and I am currently enjoying my life. Last, but definitely not least, I am a wife because I married John while he was still incarcerated when my youngest was two years old. After much soul searching, I discovered who I was and what I wanted out of life. I finally found my identity and the self-confidence that I was missing, and the love I thought I'd never have again. I am looking forward to beginning the next chapter of life when John is released at the end of this year.

Kesha "The Confidence Converter" Jackson, LPC

Kesha Jackson is the owner of All Eyez On Me Life Coaching and Counseling Services LLC, which is a company she initially designed to provide emotional support services to children ages five to twelve to assist them in overcoming the long-term effects of bullying. She then took the company to a different level and began offering her services to adults and corporations.

Kesha works intensely with others on enhancing inner strengths and abilities to increase their levels of self-esteem. Through person to person contact or online- digital secure methods she incorporates life coaching techniques and therapeutic approaches to guide others through her program modules that include: positive self –image, modeling, positive self-talk, law of attraction and other spiritual remedies. Clients are assisted in developing levels of self-confidence needed to motivate them and thrust them emotionally forward so that they can feel assured in their ability to live their best lives and move beyond any feelings of inadequacy.

She consults with businesses and facilitates organizational trainings on the little-known and detrimental effects of workplace bullying and the importance of improving production and work satisfaction through employees who feel more confident in themselves and their ability to add value to the companies that they work for. She is a wife, a mother to four beautiful children as well as a therapeutic host home parent for children in the Western Pennsylvania foster care system. She is the author of *The Change in Me from the Reflections I See*. Kesha is extremely creative in her methods of getting clients to positively focus on themselves and she sincerely delights in helping others get to the next level in life. When clients, family, and friends want help in releasing their awesome potential and becoming their magnificent selves they call Kesha "The Confidence Converter."

Visit www.confidenceconverter.com for more contact information and treatment services available.

CHAPTER ELEVEN:
Grieving with Grit, Grace, and Gratitude

Alyssa Gavulic, PhD, LMHC, LMFT

Widowed, death of a child, suicide, homicide, dementia, old age, and cancer. That list truly seems like a lifetime of suffering and loss not meant to be endured by just one person—let alone to have occurred in less than five years. But that is my story.

It all started abruptly when I became a special operations military widow with six children at the age of thirty-three after my husband of fifteen years, Joshua, died in a freefall parachute training accident. The nation honored our family's sacrifice, called my late husband a hero, wrote articles highlighting his achievements, and even handed me a folded flag as a symbol of their gratitude. But that didn't do much to change the fact that the love of my life, my best friend, and the father of my children would no longer be a part of my world.

So, as any other newly trained clinician would do, I sought out every educational, emotional, spiritual, and social resource I could. I started personal psychotherapy, read countless books, deepened and expanded my faith, journaled to make sense of my thoughts and emotions, attended grief groups, drew close to my family and friends, participated in a variety of memorials, and engaged in diverse new life affirming activities as I tried to process my intense grief. While nothing seemed to adequately soothe the sense of deep sorrow and gnawing desperation I had as I faced this new reality, I marked days off the calendar and filled every moment with intention. Rather than treating grief as the delicate process it is, I anxiously pushed through my grief by counting minutes and keeping momentum.

Then, just after I had gotten through the one-year anniversary of my husband's death, I tragically lost my two-and-a-half-year-old daughter, Lylah, in a drowning accident. She was lost so unexpectedly that any progress that I thought I had made in healing was now completely convoluted by adding the unfathomable heartache of losing my daughter too. Grief washed over me in waves of relentless emotion as I tried to survive the anguish of these two close and personal devastating losses. When a mother outlives her own child, it is just so aversive to the senses that shock and protest seem to stubbornly persist without relent. I remember weeping uncontrollably several times and deliberating about who I would cry for at that moment because I knew that my heart just couldn't handle both at once.

In an attempt to create some distance between myself and the reminders of my pain, my five surviving children and I relocated to another state. But we quickly found that you cannot outrun grief and you certainly cannot avoid ever encountering it again, when just six months later, my brother, Mitchell, died by suicide after an extensive battle with depression and addiction. My distraught family and I instinctively began to collectively search for those hidden indications and thus elusive opportunities to which we might have responded to prevent this untimely death. But none of the answers we found would ever reconcile the eternal ambiguities that will forever keep the mind at odds with the heart in accepting this kind of loss.

Assuming we must be due for some reprieve, my family and I were outraged when less than a year later, my youngest brother, Matthew, was murdered in a federally investigated quadruple homicide that was committed during a burglary and covered up by arson. We all had to fight fiercely not to be consumed in the resentment, anger, and unforgiveness that often accompanies losses that involve such a definitive element of selfish human choice. Again, we discovered that even when his murderers were found and justice was supposedly served, the closure didn't alleviate the gaping chasm in our hearts that animosity kept trying to fill.

Grieving had unwelcomely become a way of life for me. But I soon learned that loss can come in many forms and each has its own unique grieving process. When my grandmother, Mimi, died of dementia at seventy-three less than a year later, I learned that sometimes grief begins before someone is even gone because they are no longer who they once were. When my grandfather, Forest, followed her out of this life just six months later dying of old-age and a broken heart at ninety-three, I learned that although some deaths are more natural, more expected, and maybe even easier to accept—they still do not lose their sting. In fact, when my best friend, Lila, was diagnosed with breast cancer six months later and had to concede to losing a part of her own body to a double mastectomy to survive, I learned that some partial losses can even be welcomed eagerly over the alternative but must still be grieved all the same.

Most would be overwhelmed, exhausted, perplexed and even traumatized by all that I have been through. But instead of succumbing irrevocably to the despair that often wrestles for prominence when evaluating such extensive losses, I chose to tenaciously hold on to the hope that healing would eventually come. After all, if I couldn't maintain my genuine belief in the stubborn resilience of the human spirit, how could I remain authentic as a purveyor of hope and facilitator of healing in the therapeutic profession? As each layer of the shock, denial, anger, questioning, and acceptance in my grief journey unfolded, I acknowledged that I needed to make a conscious choice. Would I try to work through my grief in a way that separated my personal story from my work as a clinician? Or would I allow my pain to be a conduit for showing empathy and healing to others? I chose the latter.

So, in my determination to make meaning out of and find purpose in these life-altering experiences, I initiated a PhD about six months after my husband died and ambitiously completed it concurrently with these losses in three-and-a-half years. I resolved to not only research resilience and posttraumatic growth as comprehensively as I could, but to authentically live out a narrative of overcoming in every facet of my life. Ironically, however, as I tenaciously pursued the line of research that I thought would show me the most efficient and effective trajectory out of suffering, I kept finding myself having to appreciate the beautiful complexities of sitting in the depths of the pain first. After all, we can't be resilient or have posttraumatic growth if we do not first have some form of suffering, pain, or crisis that evokes that response. Ultimately, all my studies culminated in a dissertation on how humans view, make sense of, and most remarkably—overcome their suffering. That process became an extraordinary dance between emotional subjectivity, intellectual objectivity, and integrative reflection as I sought to articulate academically a process that I was so vividly living out experientially.

In the midst of all of these tragedies and transitions, I also continued to work as a licensed psychotherapist and marriage and family therapist. But my work in this arena would undoubtedly be forever altered. I could no longer approach my clients with the naïve optimism of a new clinician that views problems merely through the lens of case conceptualization and treatment plans. I have been in my own experiences of suffering long enough to know that what we need most in these frightening, confusing, and overwhelmingly hard places in life is to be compassionately seen by another, extended the safe space to authentically process how we are experiencing it, and be given genuine hope that we can and will eventually get through it.

So, I would sit with individuals struggling to find their identity in major life transitions and empathize more deeply after having to recreate my own identity when the life I planned withered into ashes in my grasping hands. I would sit with individuals who had anxiety and/or depression and empathize more deeply after having to manage unpredictable emotions that either amped up or shut down my own nervous system. I would sit with couples who at the core of their self-defeating cycles just feared losing each other and empathize more deeply after having had to let go of someone I was not prepared to lose. I would sit with individuals as they wrestled with existential questions and empathize more deeply after having come to the end of my own understanding and found myself unsatisfied with the irreconcilable truths of human existence we are all forced to accept.

I think it is important to state here, however, that I wasn't ready to see clients in bereavement until I had processed my own grief. I knew that I needed to find enough clarity and temporal distance from my losses to be able to see the possible trajectories, complications, and resolutions that may come after these types of events. I had to wait to make sure that enough healing had come for my own heart that I could use my experiences to deeply empathize and bravely enter into another's pain with them without forgetting that it is the client who I am being present for in those moments of compassion and connection.

Eventually, I would also sit openly with people in various stages of deep grief and reverently hold space for their pain while differentially holding sanctuary for my pain too. Although I acknowledge that each grief experience is incredibly unique, I feel I can empathize with each person's experience of suffering from a depth that resonates in my bones. I learned to personally and professionally honor the existentially and emotionally complicated process of grieving. I learned to companion the grieving through this long and arduous journey in a way that is more about being with and less about moving through. I learned to lean into the poignant vulnerability that saturates us in unpredictable waves of emotions such as denial, longing, questioning, protest, acceptance and even eventually and most exquisitely—gratitude. I learned to appreciate with awe and wonder how something as fragile the human heart can be expanded through our experiences of suffering to sometimes even hold all these feelings simultaneously.

I now sit with the widow/widower who lost his/her spouse and empathize with them as they have to learn to live their life incessantly being temporally pushed forward by time while holding vigil in their heart for the longing their person's loss left behind. I sit with the grieving mothers/fathers and empathize as they try to accept the audacity of their life's story to include their child being taken from them. I sit with suicide survivors and empathize with the struggle to let the mind's questions be filtered by their heart's ache as they think of the one they will forever miss. I sit with survivors of homicide and empathize with the frustration of screaming out for justice at the thought of who was stolen from their violated life plan but being left with the void of them still being gone in the end. I sit with caregivers of those with dementia/Alzheimer's and empathize with the confusion that comes when we lose our loved ones inside of their own fragile aging minds long before they leave this life. I sit with those who lost someone after a long fulfilling life and empathize with how they still end up feeling like our loved ones, regardless of age, are something our hearts were never meant to lose.

Finally, reader, I sit with you and empathize with how hard it is to lean into living fully knowing the loss that has already or will eventually have to enter in. It is true, loving deeply does open us up to the possibility of heartache and grief unspeakable but how else would we ever experience wholeheartedness and wordless moments of contented bliss? So choose to love deeply anyway because I can promise you this - I would rather have loved hard and lost so many knowing I loved them with my whole heart than to look back and wish I would have loved them harder when I had the chance.

Alyssa Gavulic, PhD, LMHC, LMFT

Alyssa Gavulic is a licensed mental health counselor and a licensed marriage and family therapist with a PhD in Counseling Education and Supervision. She completed her dissertation on *Examining the Effect of Parental Attachment, Emotional Maturity, Spiritual Maturity, and View of Suffering on Sense of Coherence* and is on an active research team investigating various dimensions of resilience in relation to diverse life experiences.

Alyssa is the director of Crosspoint Counseling Center in Niceville, FL, and practices as a psychotherapist that specializes in resiliency, wellness, interpersonal neurobiology, trauma recovery, relational dynamics, emotional competence, personality patterns, military stressors, and bereavement counseling.

Co-authored and Compiled by Jacqueline Rech

PART TWO

"If you can't fly, then run, if you can't run, then walk, if you can't walk, then crawl, but by all means keep moving." [3]

– MARTIN LUTHER KING JR.

Co-authored and Compiled by Jacqueline Rech

CHAPTER ONE:

The Potter's Wheel

*"Although the world is full of suffering,
it is also full of the overcoming of it."* [4]

- HELEN KELLER

    I would consider myself an artistic person. I have used drawing, painting, photography, and I tried out interpretive dance once in college just for fun. One thing I have never tried is pottery. When I think of this art form my mind wanders to that scene in the movie *Ghost*. You know the one: hands are moving together in beautifully flowing motions. There is dramatic music playing and the whole thing is romanticized for our enjoyment. But you know what other thing comes to mind? The pounding and shaping of the clay (sometimes with sharp instruments), selecting and mixing the paint or glaze, and the time it takes to fire up the kiln to intense temperatures in order to bake this creation and allow it to cool. Only after this long and labor-intensive process are we left with something that is both strong and fragile, decorative and useful. The clay started its life deep within the earth before it was dug out and shaped on a potter's wheel. That wheel is the stage we call life, and the pounding, and scraping, and molding are the results of our life experiences. Of course, clay doesn't feel the pain of the process like we do, but the results are just as beautiful.

I want you to know that your life experiences, as painful as they have been, did not only cut into your heart, soul, mind, and body, but they made you and shaped you into the person you are today. And the person you are today is brave and beautiful. You are a survivor. You are worthy of love, and friendship, and healing. But I feel the need to add that you did not *need* the abusive situation or trauma, nor the abusive person(s) to *become* who you are today. These situations and persons do not get to take credit for one iota of the strength you possess and have used to overcome so much. Just as every pebble, and stone changes the trajectory of the water in a river, so have your experiences changed the course of your life and shaped you. You may have ended up someplace you weren't expecting due to these circumstances or events. You may even be stuck in a cycle full of shame, and regret. However, I hope you are able recognize the amount of strength, and grit it took for you to get here today. Look at how much you've already overcome! That is what I want to focus on in this chapter.

But how do you heal from all that trauma, abuse, loss, and brokenness? What meaning do your painful experiences hold that shaped you into who you are today?

Growing up, I was never able to process and understand the trauma I experienced. For most of my life, I felt as though I was adrift in the ocean being tossed to and fro, and doing everything I could to stay afloat and avoid being eaten by some terrifying creature just under the surface waiting to devour me. I struggled through each wave of traumatic experience as it washed over me, and braced myself for the next wave I knew was inevitably coming. It wasn't until I was an adult and went through years of processing through these experiences did I feel my feet on solid ground for the first time. But until then my days and years were filled with the tension your mind and body hold as it braces for the impact of the unknown.

My earliest impacts began before exiting the womb when my biological mother, according to her mother, visited an abortion clinic. She was too 'freaked out' to go through with the process, though this did not stop her from attempting to end her pregnancy at home. Thankfully her plans did not prevail and instead, resulted in my very premature birth. I spent months fighting to live at the onset of my existence, an experience that set the tone for the rest of my life. I spent the first few years of my life in neglect by a mother who experienced some trauma herself, while my father shuttled us around Air Force bases across the country. I shared about the trauma that had me seeing myself from behind. I would come to learn the term for this as dissociation, and it was my tiny little body's way of trying to protect my mind. After this time, we were sent to live with various family members, and then with our father until he reached out to child services for help. It was then that we entered the foster care system until our father was able to provide a better living situation for us. As well-intentioned as our foster mother was, she still could not protect us from the impactful situations we experienced while in her care at the hands of our foster brother. By the age of eight, I had moved eleven times, lived in three states, and attended three schools. This set me up for a life of struggling to form healthy relationships and friendships, searching for a mother figure, and fighting against depression and rejection, while searching for some stability in life. This searching part of my life included moving a total of thirty-six times, marrying three times (two marriages to men struggling to deal with their own issues), and experiencing a whole host of traumatic experiences, abuse, and loss.

I share this with you because I know what it is like to feel broken, used up, abandoned, and rejected. I know what it is like to feel so ugly and disfigured from life it seems like no one could possibly love, or even want to befriend me. I know what it feels like to walk into a room full of 'normal' people and feel as though my flesh is gaping wide open and the entrails of my past trauma are spilling out for all to see and gawk at like some mangled carnage on the side of a freeway. I know what it feels like to be a square peg in a round hole and feel all alone.

But here's the thing: I wasn't alone. And neither are you.

Yes, I know you might 'technically' be alone. You are living your own unique life and may not have anyone to experience it with. But you are not alone in how those experiences made you feel. While working in substance abuse treatment, I had many people ask how I could possibly help them if I didn't share their *exact* experiences. My friend, I want to tell you that no one can live your *exact* experience. The fingerprint of your loss or trauma is your very own. But these experiences do leave an impression that many people can identify with. My answer to this line of questioning was always the same: I might not know the exact pain you describe, but I can tell you that I know what abandonment feels like. I know what loss, self-doubt, depression, shame, anxiety, anger, bitterness, unforgiveness, despair, violation, betrayal all *feel* like. It was those shared impressions we each had of our own human experiences that enabled me to meet the person in front of me right where they were and walk alongside them on a familiar path to healing.

It was ultimately my faith in God that was invaluable to my own healing process, and reframing, or thinking differently, about my past trauma. I also had to forgive myself (I blamed myself for suffering in both my marriages because I chose to stay), because God forgave me, and allow myself the grace to understand the mental and emotional state I was in during my many poor choices. I needed to process every trauma, move, marriage, and loss in therapy. Lastly, I had to think of myself differently, too. I discarded the victim role I held onto for far too long, and took ownership of the strength and resilience I found to survive, thrive, and give back to others.

My faith journey has been a work in progress. I'm thankful that my non-believing grandparents saw some value and worth in sending my brother and I off to church with a friendly neighbor lady. Those earliest experiences really laid the groundwork for my faith today. Even if you don't believe in God, or Jesus, or another higher power, you can probably agree that surviving takes faith. The biblical text defines faith as "being the confidence of what we hope for, the evidence of things we cannot see." (Hebrews 11:1 NIV) [5] I'd say that it took a lot of faith to believe that my outward circumstances and inner turmoil would change. I *needed* faith in a better life to come to get me through my worst days. But most importantly, I needed faith in God and trusting his plan for my life in order to sustain and maintain my sanity during the most difficult parts of my story. I hope that you would allow some kind of faith to enter your heart and mind, and that this faith would produce hope, and hope would help you persevere through your hardships right now.

My grandparents were the ones who saw value in sending my brother and me along to church on Sundays even though neither ascribed to a structured faith or belief system. A kind woman faithfully took us to and from church, which helped lay the foundation for my faith. It was God's love that sustained me through my unstable childhood, rebellious teenager, and early college years. And it was the love and support of my ex-mother-in-law which allowed my faith to grow and flourish as it is today. Experiencing God's love brought peace to my heart and mind, and restored all the broken pieces of my story. He helped me to see my story through the lens of his eyes, and that made all the difference.

During the process of seeing my story differently, I had to *think* of my story differently. One of the hardest things for me to do was to think about my experiences and not see all the trauma first. It was like looking at a body of water, unable to see myself through all the muck and debris just under the surface. I looked at my reflection and saw the gaping wounds trauma left behind and was convinced others could see them too wherever I went. But when I began thinking about all the parts of me that became stronger because of my experiences, I felt stronger. Those wounds? They began to close up and heal. I even began to appreciate the pain and give thanks for it. I began to think of it as the pain that alerts your body to much-needed changes.

Thriving takes a lot of work. It is not gained without tears, reflection, and honesty. The honesty component of that statement was quite terrifying for me. I had to be willing to acknowledge my role in my own pain, while refusing to accept responsibility for the actions of others. I discovered along this healing journey that my life experiences provided me with a depth of compassion for others, and the realization of an inner strength I never knew I possessed. My life experiences made me into the caring, hard-working, thoughtful, strong, resilient, and faithful person that I am today. These life experiences provided me with a platform from which to reach out to help others, and to write this book. Once I thought about my experiences from the point of view of strength and resilience, I was finally able to see that my life experiences didn't maim me. They made me. And your life experiences can and have done the same for you, if you can take a step back and step into your own journey of healing.

In the following chapters, I am going to challenge you to look at your life, your experiences, your attitudes towards healing, and the way you see yourself in that process. You will read all about how eleven brave and triumphant people in the first half of the book sought healing for themselves, and were able to move towards a place of health and wholeness. After each chapter, there will be reflective questions for you to take a look at and answer open and honestly, in a way that brings to light some things that you can discuss with a trusted friend, family member, or even a therapist. This book will also include a section in the back with additional resources for you. Life is a struggle, and none of us can really do life well *all* on our own as we were meant to be in community with one another. I hope you can feel the care and compassion we each have poured into this book because we had YOU in mind when we wrote it. You are important. You are worthy of wholeness. You are worth the time and effort and investment towards healing. You deserve peace. You deserve to feel loved and cared about.

Life is a journey. We do not travel alone.

So, to start off I have some questions for you. Feel free to write your answers in this book, or in a journal if you plan on passing this along to another person who could benefit from its pages.

- What are three defining moments/ time periods/ experiences in your life that are still affecting you in a negative or unhealthy way?

- How do you feel when you walk in a room full of people you deem as 'healthy and happy'?

- What are some unhealthy ways you have been coping with these experiences?

- What are some positive attributes/ character traits that you can attribute to these experiences?

CHAPTER TWO:

Kintsugi

"Our wounds are often the openings into the best and most beautiful part of us." [6]

- DAVID RICHO

I very recently discovered that I am of Japanese descent. No, it wasn't from some mail-order DNA kit. It was through social media, more specifically, Facebook. I had been searching for my biological father for nearly fifteen years without any solid or substantial leads. One day, while I was scrolling through my newsfeed, I read a post that discussed hidden message folders with filtered messages in them. So, in January of 2016, a month before I gave birth to my first child, I decided to do a little digging in my own filtered messages folder. Lo' and behold, I had a message there from a man I did not know. The message was dated for October of 2012 (just a month before I married my now husband.) To make a long story short, a DNA test revealed that he is my biological father (I guess I did do the mail-order DNA test after all) and he was born and raised in Japan. Naturally, I did what anyone would do in my situation and I began researching everything about Japan.

A few months ago, I came across a post on my social media. The image was of broken pottery that was repaired with gold. I found this to be intriguing so I did a bit of Googling and discovered that the practice is called Kintsugi [7]. This word is translated as 'golden repair'. According to the website Modern Met, the repair is done with a "special lacquer dusted with powdered gold, silver, or platinum." This kind of repair work celebrates the uniqueness and beauty the cracks and brokenness created in the piece, often making the piece even *more beautiful* than it was before the repair.

The image stuck with me for many reasons, but mostly because I could see my life story reflected in the image of the beautifully repaired piece of art. Someone had taken the time to craft this bowl or vase with their hands, and someone else had taken equal amounts of care in restoring the beauty back to the piece after it was shattered. It reminded me of ourselves, and our journeys through life. We are broken, but by the hands of a healthy support system, compassionate therapist, faith in God or other higher power, and an atmosphere of acceptance, kindness, and love we, too, can have the beauty of our lives restored. They become the golden repair that adds beauty and depth to our experiences. It takes time, but even after you've fallen you *can* get back up!

How do you feel about your own life experiences? Do you feel as though you will always be broken, damaged, and in emotional and psychological pain? Do you feel as though you could never meet or obtain the kind of caring and compassionate support that you need to move up and out of your brokenness? My hope for you is that by the end of this book, you feel seen and loved. I hope that you can take a step toward healing by sharing with someone the pain and struggle that is on the inside. I want each of you to see yourselves like vessels repaired by gold.

I know it is so hard. Today's American society and culture celebrates busy-ness, and being overbooked and overworked. Even if given the time to do so, most Americans don't use their vacation days for fear of falling behind in work, or being seen as an unmotivated employee. Independence has also become like an idol to our own detriment, requiring that we "pull ourselves up by the bootstraps," so to speak. And if we aren't able to do so, we are met with judgement, and spit out by the societal machine that only tears us down without building us back up. Rest seems to be a luxury for those who can afford to take the time away from work to invest in their own physical, mental, and emotional care. But for many, and maybe even you, time away from work means you can't pay bills, buy shoes for your child, or purchase life-saving medications which have to stay on the shelf at the pharmacy. But it is for these reasons, and many more, that our culture needs to remove the stigma against mental and emotional health care, and the people who seek treatment.

A lot of my examples from this book come from my own lived experiences, because that is all I can really pull from. Right now, I am in the thick of motherhood, rearing a one and three-year-old. My oldest wants to do everything by himself, and I allow him the opportunity to learn. I show him what he should do and give him time to practice implementing these lessons. I do not require perfection from him, but follow him along his journey as he learns to master each new skill. When I take the time to discover his goals, I can offer encouragement, instead of shame, as he tries to reach them. I position myself in a place of teacher, and encourager so that we can celebrate together when he has achieved a new milestone. The kind of atmosphere I provide my child with should be the kind of encouraging atmosphere we each are afforded when seeking help for the mental and emotional turmoil we struggle with.

Just imagine what it would be like if you had a designated place at work that you could go to have a mental health break filled with fresh air, and greenery. Or better, that your office supported counseling sessions during the last hour of the day once a week so you could be seen by a therapist while your children are still in daycare. What would it look like in your group of friends, or your family if you could openly discuss your mental and emotional health, and these same people involved in your life could have a place to be informed on how best to support you and each other? What if the phrase, "I see a therapist" wasn't fretted over before it even left your lips? What if our children were taught how to recognize and talk about their emotions, learning individual strategies to help bring them back to emotional homeostasis throughout their day? What if we didn't dismiss the concerns of the aging or elderly? What if we didn't demand that our lives be filled with happiness all the time? What if we weren't taught to fear our emotions, but accept all of them as part of the human experience, then learn to manage and express them in healthy ways? What if ...

These are all questions for us to consider as we search for ways to make and be the change we want to see. But in addition, I would like to mention the stigma within our society and culture surrounding medication for the treatment of mental and emotional illness and issues. If the stigma towards seeing a therapist is bad, then taking an anti-anything medication is even worse. There exists a voice inside our society that says, "Why do you need *that?* What's *wrong* with you?" The shame that accompanies this type of treatment is so high that many who could and do benefit from its short and/or long-term use often stop taking their medications to avoid being a statistic. However, abruptly stopping any prescribed medication could have detrimental effects.

Each person is entitled to their own views towards medication, but I would be amiss in this book if I didn't at least address the topic in a way that helps break down the stigma. Yes, there are those that would be perceived as trying to take advantage of the system, or abuse a medication. But I'm not speaking for those people. I'm speaking for the mom who cannot get herself out of bed because of her severe depression, or the young man who can't keep a job because his anxiety is so high, he spends more time rehearsing worst-case scenarios than any other activity in his day. I'm speaking for the person who would rather contemplate or attempt suicide than get the help he needs because what would the guys at work think about him? It is so easy for us to go to the doctor's office if we are sick or break a bone.

My hope is that it would become just as acceptable, or even *expected*, for someone to seek out a therapist when they need help coping with mental and emotional pain or trauma. I hope their when life feels overwhelming, when their marriage becomes chaos, when they just can't stop themselves from x, y, and z, and every scenario in between that they can openly say, "I'm getting help for that." And if I could hope beyond all hopes, I would also hope these same people would also seek out Jesus, and spiritual support in addition to professional counseling, and medical supervision. It is truly my sincere hope.

I would in no way make my small children battle an illness of theirs alone if there was a lifesaving medication that could help them. Sometimes medications give a person the break they need from their symptoms so they can have the headspace to make the best use of therapeutic interventions, and other support they receive. Medications can and do help many people for short and long term use. So, if you are in need of any medications for mental and emotional issues, I want you to know *I see you. You matter.*

Sometimes all you need around you are people who show you care and kindness, without judgement when your mind, emotions, and life are feeling completely wrecked and torn from trauma, grief, or any other experience that would leave you open and exposed. I feel blessed to have had people around me who encouraged and supported me during the many times I've fallen or found myself at my lowest points along the way. It took these same people to speak truth into my life about things that were happening in it. But also the truth of who they knew I was even if I didn't know or recognize myself. I had to accept help even if I didn't want it. For example, when I left my second husband because I knew I had nowhere to go. I spent the first three days afterwards couch-surfing at different places. Even though I was hurting at the time, I felt incredibly proud of myself for having the strength and courage to leave an unhealthy situation. Finally, a coworker of mine opened her home to me and nurtured me for an entire summer while I took the time to gather myself after such a disorienting experience. She saw that I needed help, and though I really didn't have many options, a part of me wanted to refuse her offer because I thought I should have been able to figure it out on my own. See the damage that belief system can cause? Was taking over one of her children's bedrooms while rifling through garbage bags of my clothes an ideal situation? No. Was I already hurting and ashamed? Yes. But did I need her help, and the truth she spoke into my heart and mind after my experience? Most definitely, without a doubt.

It is important that you know it's okay to get back up at your own speed. This isn't a race. And your healing journey doesn't have to look any certain kind of way. As long as you continue taking steps toward healthy boundaries and emotional self-regulation; continue to surround yourself with people that care for and nurture your healing, and continue to engage in the work it takes to reach your full potential, then it does not matter how long it takes you. Honestly, we all will be in a state of moving toward healing in some or many areas, and maintaining health in others, for the rest of our lives. Give yourself permission to heal at your own speed. Don't compare yourself and healing journey to others' expectations of what you should be doing or achieving. It's okay to stop that unhealthy thing you're doing and completely reinvent yourself. It's even okay to attempt that process and fail, but then course correct and try again. Don't be afraid to fail. Failure is not our enemy or even something to be identified by. All perceived failures in life are just ways of learning what doesn't work or serve us in our goal of healing. That's all. Who doesn't like to learn a better way of doing things? You can only learn what works better if you already know what doesn't work well. And the process by which you discover what doesn't work well is called learning, not failure. So, I would like to correct my previous statement. Don't be afraid to *learn*. And while you're learning, why don't you get back up and try again?

There's no one size fits all answer to that question. I can tell you that finding it worthwhile to get back up is a good place to start. Take a few minutes to answer the questions below. I've left space in the book for you to write in:

- What do I struggle most in my day to day functioning when it comes to the life experience or trauma I wrote about in Chapter One? (Lack of support, lack of time, lack of healthcare or money for appointments, stressful work environment, toxic relationships, etc.)

- What are some of the messages I have received through social media, family, friends, etc. when it comes to seeking out mental and emotional health care?

- Who can I talk to about how I'm feeling? Can I call, text, email, or visit them right now if I needed to?

- When was the last time you tried something new and failed? How did you get back up? And what did you learn in the process? (No matter how small the failure or victory.)

If you don't have the support you need, I want you to continue reading. This healing journey is one that is going to require you to get outside of your comfort zone. It may even require that you reach out to people you haven't spoken to in years. You may feel broken, defeated, and worthless. But like all those pieces of pottery, you are worth saving. Your brokenness can become your greatest strength and beauty. I hope you'll continue this journey with me through the rest of this book.

CHAPTER THREE:

Healing is a Verb

"We can and should feel confident enough to take ourselves on as worthy projects." [8]

- CATHY BURNHAM MARTIN

As I mentioned earlier, I am a young mother. And by young, I mean my children are young and I have yet to reach an expert level in parenting. My world consists of diaper changes, dinosaur-shaped foodstuffs, and songs about baby animals that I dare not repeat lest they become lodged in my cranium for all of eternity. I am a mother, and my children are, well, my children. And when one of them become hurt, it is my job to scoop them up. Healing happens passively for them. They nuzzle into me, and I spend as much time as they need simply holding them, providing loving and reassuring touch and sounds to help them feel safe and cared for. I kiss boo-boos, apply bandages, and send them off to continue whatever adventure awaits them. Their healing has begun, and will continue until it is complete. But they are children, with physical wounds. We are adults, and some of us have experienced mental and emotional traumas that can't be contained in the arms of someone we trust and love. And they certainly can't be fixed with a bandage.

My family and I try to see the ocean once a year. But last year our vacation was cut short by the oncoming hurricane that was barreling straight for us. We made several calls to the airline, spoke to many customer service agents for hours, and were finally able to purchase flights to escape the storm we saw coming. But there are storms, or fires and other disasters that many do not see coming. I can think of a particular town in Northern California that no longer exists. You can find its location on a map, but the town itself was decimated by fire. Its nearly 27,000 townspeople [9] left without homes, without their loved ones and beloved animals, their livelihoods, or any semblance of what was before the devastation occurred [10]. At the time of this writing, they have yet to return to their town to start rebuilding, nearly six months later. They couldn't anticipate or prevent such devastation, and neither could you foresee nor prevent the traumatic event or experience had you endured. Trauma leaves our hearts and minds and souls scorched, much like the grounds this peaceful town sat on. Unrecognizable in any light. The way back to healing and reconstruction a seemingly overwhelming process, but not impossible.

Healing is a verb, and it doesn't happen on its own. There is no one to assuage the turmoil that roils inside of us. There is no one here on this earth that can hold in all the sadness, shock, and pain of the preceding years within their embrace. There is just you, and just me, lost in the constant replay of past events with two questions to ask: Do I want to heal? Am I willing to take ownership for what that process might entail? If the answer to both of those questions is "yes" then first, I need you to press PAUSE on the replay. I don't say STOP because only time and healing can truly stop the unwanted replay of what we didn't ask for in the first place. But you can give yourself permission to pause, take a deep breath, and rest. In fact, why don't you take a moment to do that now? I want you to close your eyes, and clear your mind. Focus on the sounds around you, the sensation of the seat beneath you. You might even imagine a far-off place with a warm and gentle breeze. Breathe in deeply through your nose for a slow count of three, and exhale completely through your mouth. Feel that cool air entering your lungs and fill them to capacity, and your shoulders and chest relax as the air is expelled from your body. One more time. And lastly, again. How do you feel? Do you know what you just did right there? You made the conscious choice to pause, to act, and to wait. You did that. Not the person sitting in the room with you, or your fur baby who is demanding their next meal. And you know what?

Your healing can simply start there. Right there where you are. In that comfy spot you're sitting in reading this book. If you decided to choose healing, then you are already on that path!

"But what if I'm not ready for healing? What if I'm not ready to do all of the things, or say all of the words?" Those are some excellent

questions, and it is totally okay if you aren't ready. I catch myself wanting to shake my fist at my biological mother all. the. time. That part of my house is still a work in progress (more on that later). After all, you've probably picked up this book because you thought it might be interesting to hear all kinds of stories from therapists, or maybe a friend handed you a copy and you put it in your bag and forgot about it. And you certainly weren't expecting to be making any life-altering decisions that require you to take a look at something that you would rather leave at the bottom of the proverbial pile. I get it. And I hear you. But I also care about you, and have shed tears writing these words (really, I cried today in the library I'm sitting at this very moment because YOU are the reason why I began this journey.) So, I'd like to respect your place in your journey to healing and give you some things to think about. No harm in reading *about* healing, right?

You see, I already mentioned above that healing is a verb. It has been a long time since I have had to study the English language, so when I looked up the definition of active and passive verbs, I realize that healing is *both*. When you choose to engage in the healing process, you are choosing to act and initiate the healing. But you are also the receiver of the healing, whether by your own hand or by the hand of someone else (in my case, God). And if I can imagine the whole complicated healing process, I would use the illustration of rebuilding a home.

Trauma is like the lava that spews from within the earth's core. The only thing it can do at the time is to destroy anything and everything in its path. It comes and destroys your home, and the peace you had hold of inside that home with you. But lava cools and hardens and leaves a path for new things to grow, and new homes to be built.

Imagine for a moment that healing from your pain and trauma is like building a home for yourself. This is the place where new memories will develop and come to live alongside you. I have never personally been in the process of building a brand-new home, but I can tell you about a few friends who have invited me into that process via their Instagram page or Facebook stories. It is fascinating to me. And of course, if you are anything like me you could probably spend hours on a weekend binge-watching reruns of *Fixer Upper* (seriously, Jo, I think you are a domestic and spatial genius, even though I'm still waiting for you to come visit *my* home). The building (or in this case, rebuilding) process takes *time* and *intention*. Using this analogy, when I think about all the time I spent *not* getting the help I needed to begin rebuilding my house of healing, I imagine being a squatter on the land where my house once stood. Struggling to have my basic needs met, weathering the storms of life as they come without any resilience and protection. Just surviving, but not thriving. But because I care for you, I want you to THRIVE in your healing journey!

The first step would be to recognize that you need help, and that healing isn't going to happen on its own. It is deciding to take a step forward, however small, and *choosing* to keep taking steps forward each and every day regardless of what your fear, shame, anxiety, self-doubt, and depression tell you. You are stronger than you think! Building a solid foundation is essential for healing to begin. It requires going through your plot of land and clearing away all the weeds, small trees, and anything else that has grown since your trauma happened. For many people, this looks like challenging their long-held beliefs about themselves and their ability to heal and move forward. It looks like accepting your own worth and value as a human being, and deciding you are worthy of healing. Then, taking the first step may be reaching out to a friend to talk about what it is you are going through, or giving one of us a call in the profession to schedule an appointment. And even though we can come alongside you to make plans and blueprints, it's ultimately you who needs to build your own house. Time and intention, remember?

Some pillars of a strong foundation of healing:

- **Grace**

    Grace allows you to go easy on yourself when you're learning something brand new. And guess what? Healing, and rebuilding a healthy life with healthy relationships and responses to your environment might be something brand new to you. You would not expect perfection from a toddler just learning to walk. You would not line this wee little one next to an Olympic runner, and expect them to win, right? So, allow yourself some grace for the day. Take a deep breath and continue forward even if you stumble or fall.

- **Forgiveness**

    This is a huge one. Because I'm not talking about the person or group that has hurled abuse and pain your way, though forgiving them in the process is important, but I'm talking about you. Yes, *you*. I'm asking you to be open to forgiving *yourself* for whatever blame you have accepted for whatever pain you have caused, or more importantly *not* caused. And while you're at it, can you try to stop the "should haves" and "could haves" and "what ifs" from leaving your mouth or entering your mind? That's called bargaining, and there isn't anything you can do about what has already happened. But what you CAN do RIGHT NOW is decide on a future filled with healing and move forward with grace and forgiveness.

- **Courage**

I am so proud of you! Really, I am! You are reading this book and really thinking about some of the things inside. You might have already decided that you want to embark on your own healing journey and build one of those houses you just read about. All of that takes courage, and if you've made the decision to seek healing then you, my friend, are COURAGEOUS. If you don't feel courageous right now, that's okay too. I had to borrow courage from people around me before I could believe it for myself. You can borrow my courage, if you need it. I'll be happy to lend it to you.

- **Patience**

Like expecting a toddler to best an Olympic athlete, expecting your house to be built and your journey towards healing to be accomplished in a couple of counseling sessions, or a short length of time is unreasonable and unrealistic. It took me *years* of weekly counseling sessions to process through all my trauma, fears, and everything else. Years. And I'm still on that journey. I will continue to learn and grow from my experiences and pass along that growth for the entire rest of my life. I wouldn't want it to be any other way. Remember, healing takes *time* and *intention.*

- **Safe Support(s)**

You might not have any of these people in your life right now. There is a section in the back of the book that might provide you with a good starting place to get some help you need. There's also a whole chapter after this one that discusses this in more detail. But it absolutely takes a village to help prop you up when you first begin your healing journey. Think of the herd, and how much safer it is for a wounded member to heal surrounded by support. Now think of that same wounded member alone in the open, and you can begin to understand the importance of safe supports in your life. Reach out to someone, anyone that you know and can trust.

- **Faith**

This is an essential part of healing. It requires that you picture in your mind a different life for yourself than what you are currently living, or have lived in the past. It takes creativity and resilience to trust in the process, to trust in God or your higher power, that what has been started can and will result in a different way of life for you. Oftentimes, you will find your 'why' in the midst of having faith for the healing that has yet to come. Hold onto your 'why'.

- **Consistency**

    This is the hardest of all these pillars. Listen, I get it. I can barely remember to get all my own fruits and vegetables in my day or week for myself, let alone for two little people. But when it came to my healing journey, one thing that really helped me stay consistent and accountable was to remember my 'why'. I reminded myself daily that I already tried going it alone, and my own feeble attempts at healing were terrible. I had no accountability, no encouragement, just me wandering the wastelands of my trauma trying to grasp anything that I thought might 'help'. But what I needed was lasting help, and support. And I needed to seek after the kind of care I needed on a daily and weekly basis. Sure, unexpected things happen and require our time and attention. But please don't give up seeking help with this part, especially when you start to feel better. It takes time, intention, *and* commitment.

So, you decided to seek out therapy and challenge some faulty thinking, and have opened up some trusted supports. You've been working hard at remaining consistent for about six months and are starting to see the beginnings of a solid foundation for healing. You and your therapist worked hard at clearing away the brush, and unhealthy things that grew in the place of hurt. You feel stronger, and better able to examine and look at your situation and circumstances. You feel better about going to talk to someone every week or so. You've been able to talk to others about the fact that you're giving yourself time to heal. And as long as you continue to be intentional throughout this process, you, your therapist, and support system can continue to help you rebuild the house that once was lost to tragedy, pain, heartache, death, and/or trauma. Day by day. Hour by hour. Minute by minute. Remember, this is the place where you will live and thrive. You wouldn't give up on building your physical home, so I hope you would stay the course and not give up on your active healing journey.

But with all best-laid plans, there are things along the building process that can and will cause delays. And if you aren't looking out for them, they could cause destruction of what you've built and accomplished.

Some blocks or hazards to healing:

- **Criticism/ Perfectionism**

    You just need to start building. Come up with a plan and move forward. Your house doesn't have to be perfect. In fact, if you don't have any experience with building a house, I can almost guarantee that it's not going to look anything like you thought it would. But that's okay, because you're taking action. And one day your home can be as beautiful and majestic as you want it to be. But for now, it just needs to be safe, and dry and provide you a place of rest.

- **Lack of positive supports**

    This is a tough one. Yes, you can 'go it alone' surprisingly far, but only so far. Eventually, you will fatigue and stop, or worse, want to go back. You will need someone along this journey with you. Our digital age makes it a bit easier to find support. But more on that later.

- **Remaining in toxic surroundings**

    This one is also a tough one, because I know there is someone reading this that has to lock themselves in a room to have a hope of being safe. You're in the midst of your trauma and turmoil. You literally do not have a safe place to begin the healing process. Your safety is of utmost importance. There are some resources in the back of this book that might help give you a starting point. But if you've reached a place where you can begin healing, you're going to need to figure out how to seek out space away from toxic people and surroundings to heal. This is where going away to a therapist's office can be of vital importance in your healing journey.

- **Holding onto toxic and/or, self-deprecating thoughts**

    Listen, I get it. You've done some terrible things. Or been told some atrocious things about yourself that may or may not be true. But you cannot continue to hold onto those things and successfully move through this healing journey. They will stop your efforts every time and push you closer and closer to the edge of giving up or going back. Neither of those two options is something you really want. Sure, giving up and going back always *seem* easier, or even better. But once you begin to taste freedom from your old way of thinking, feeling, or being, you want more of that. So, I hope you stop believing and holding onto these things about yourself, and begin to see the strength and dignity you possess.

- **Ignoring signs of relapse into negative self-talk/ unhealthy coping behaviors**

    I've heard it said that if you have to hide it from others, it's probably not serving you well. This goes for food, spending behaviors, emotional or physically intimate affairs, self-harm, anger towards your family when no one else can see, withholding the truth in any form, getting lost in fantasy by books, gaming, websites, etc. the list goes on. If you are engaging in these behaviors, then I hope you can open up about them to someone you know and trust and seek help. Also, slipping into negative self-talk is something that can keep you from progressing. Constantly reminding yourself of the pain or injustice you've been through, or putting yourself down all the time is not healthy. You would not say those things to someone you love and care about, so please try not to say them to yourself.

- **Unforgiveness**

    This is a big one. Unforgiveness is like a cancer of the heart and soul. It acts as a snare for bitterness and anger. It can absolutely manifest itself physically in your body in the form of aches and pains, gastrointestinal issues, etc. Forgiveness doesn't have to happen immediately, but being open to letting go of all that anger and bitterness can only help serve your healing process and provide you with some peace. Forgiveness allows you to take back power from those who have wronged or harmed you so you can live more freely.

- **Holding onto the victim identity**

    This is probably the toughest of them all, because you *were* a victim at some point, maybe many times over or currently. But in order to step into the healing process, you must be willing to let go of this identity and transform it into one of empowerment. You see, as a victim, you hold the weight of your anger, bitterness, resentment, and unforgiveness. Holding onto this identity is like putting blinders on. All you can see are the motives of others *against* you. Your mind and body are always on high alert for an attack or slight by others which does not help you to seek and find trusted and healthy supports along this journey. This identity may fade with time and healing, and may be the last to go. But I urge you to examine where your identity lies.

So how do you nurture the healthy foundational attributes, and guard against the unhealthy, self-sabotaging traits that may destroy the foundation of healing you have worked so hard to build? Firstly, I'd like you to know that you can take as much time as you need to rebuild and heal. Secondly, comparison is the thief of joy, as I've heard, and though this process can and most likely will be difficult, you can still find joy if you're looking for it. Please do not compare your healing journey to anyone else's. Each person's journey is just as unique as they and their lived experiences are. But every victory, no matter how small, is still a victory. And it requires that you *do something.* I am very much channeling my inner Fred Rogers (I'm even wearing a cardigan as I type this chapter). Growing up, Mr. Rogers was the penultimate encourager and educator. He taught me about emotions, and difficult situations in a way that I could digest and put into practice. Above all, he helped me feel loved, cared about, and encouraged through life. So, I'd like to be your Fred Rogers, though no one can truly fill his shoes. I know this chapter was a pretty long one, but it's important for you to understand that healing takes time. It takes intention. There will be roadblocks along the way, but if you are willing to commit to the journey, I promise you will end up where you want and need to be.

You're making it through this book, slowly and steadily. I don't want to overwhelm you with information, but I do want you to begin the process of dusting off some of those old ways of thinking. I'd like you to consider dipping your toe into the work that you may encounter when you reach out for help one day. Not too bad, right? Read on for this chapter's questions.

- What is something about this chapter that stuck out to you?

- What are two pillars of a strong foundation that you struggle with? And why?

- What are two hazards to healing you struggle with? And why?

CHAPTER FOUR:

It Takes a Village

"Anything that's human is mentionable, and anything that is mentionable can be more manageable. When we can talk about our feelings, they become less overwhelming, less upsetting, and less scary. The people we trust with that important talk can help us know that we are not alone." [11]

- FRED ROGERS

Being a first-born child, I used to think I could do everything on my own. There's a photo of me hanging in my home that documents the moment I decided to walk out the door and into the world by myself. I looked to be about a year old or younger, and I had a bottle with me. The question I asked my dad when I saw it for the first time was "you let me walk out of the house alone? And you took a picture of me instead of making sure I didn't fall down the steps?!" This was of course before cell phones equipped with cameras so my father would have had to see what was happening, recall where he placed his 35MM disposable camera, stepped over me through the doorway to the other side, and then snapped the photo. What the photo did not show was the countless hours, days, and weeks I spent mastering the skill of walking. Nor did I accomplish the task on my own. I have to assume that one or both of my parents set aside what they were doing at that moment to take me by the hand and lead me along my path. They were there for me when I fell, and bandaged my scraped knees. They encouraged me when I decided I would rather stay on the ground and cry. They did not let me give up. How do I know this? Because I walk with confidence today. I have mastered this skill and I know the work it took someone to help me learn because it is the same process I have experienced in helping my own children learn to walk.

Healing is like a journey of mastering the skill of walking on your own two feet. It takes courage and perseverance. It takes patience with yourself and grace. It takes a village around you feeding your soul with the nourishment that encouragement and love provides.

This week has been a challenge for our family as my husband has worked almost eighty hours over the span of five days. It is Saturday and I have slept a total of nineteen hours since last Sunday. My poor husband has come home just long enough to grab a few hours of sleep before he is back at it again helping to save the world. This meant that I had to be on mom duty around the clock. My children were like whack-a-mole, each taking turns waking the other up and both screaming for their father. I woke up today knowing my husband was going to work straight through the night and weekend, and I felt broken. I felt like I could not continue on this mom path. I felt alone and without support. But then a miracle happened: the cavalry arrived. First, it was my stepmother, who made the three-hour round-trip drive to sit with my children while I attended some video conference meetings. When she left, a friend decided to drop off a goodie bag of chocolate and facial masks because she knew what I needed. Lastly, a woman in a local community group, whom I have never met or spoken to in real life showed up at our doorstep with her elementary-aged daughter and two babysitters. As I sit here and type this chapter, they are downstairs cleaning my house, making dinner, and caring for my children. I am in awe of the generosity of my community. My village. And it is nothing like I thought it would look like.

That is the beauty of your support system. It doesn't have to look like what you imagined it would. Some of you reading this book right now may feel heartbroken because your support system is missing, some of the people you were counting on to be there for you aren't. I hear you, I do. You may also be thinking, *Jackie, I spent my entire life running, hiding, using, and moving. I don't have a village.* Or, *I have tried reaching out to neighbors, colleagues, family, and even strangers and have either been ignored or used and left abandoned.* I've been there, too. Thankfully, we live in a digital age where we can meet and connect with whole groups of people that we may not have had access to otherwise. Though digital networks come with pros and cons.

Some of your best friends might be people whom you've never met in real life. These are the friends that provide you a safe, judgement-free zone to vent, cry, and keep each other accountable. They've sent care packages, or a funny .gif (these are by far my most favorite love language, if a .gif could be a love language). And now, in our digital age, we can even receive therapeutic services through online forums. It was online forums like Facebook support groups that were invaluable to me while feeling alone and suffering the devastating effects of postpartum depression and anxiety. I didn't feel alone in what I was experiencing.

When my second was born, I was prepared for a rebound of the postpartum anxiety I experienced with my first but what I was unprepared for was a debilitating battle with postpartum depression. It took months for me to even recognize the symptoms in myself. I hardly left the house, I wasn't sleeping even though my children were sleeping in twelve-hour stretches, I was barely caring for my own basic needs. I was down to my pre-pregnancy weight in a couple short weeks rather than the months it took the first time. I was a mess. All I could do was cry in the basement because I didn't want to wake the kids. I told a friend how I was feeling, and she recommended a therapist that specializes in maternal mental health issues. And the best part? She could meet me online. When I was in grad school, we had discussions about the future of therapy. Everyone immediately pointed to tele and online therapy. We discussed the ethical dilemmas and implications with that treatment modality. Years later, I was working in a private practice and we offered online therapy but only by a supervisor and it wasn't covered under insurance. Clients paid cash, and only certain therapists were trained using the interface. Now, a few years later and online therapy is a reality. I contacted my insurance company and discovered that not only did my plan have coverage for virtual therapy, but I had *unlimited coverage* at only $15 per session. Wow. I was amazed at how far we, as a profession, had come in this area in such a relatively short amount of time.

While my daughter napped, and my son had his quiet time in the afternoon I met my therapist online from the comfort of my own home. It was wonderful. There was even an app I could use to access her online office, and a few times I needed to see her over my phone while the kids napped in their car seats and I parked. Postpartum depression did not care that I was a licensed professional counselor. It didn't care that my children needed their mother to be healthy and whole. It. Did. Not. Care. Postpartum depression and any other mental illness or emotional trauma do not discriminate. It could not be prevented. It just happened, and I needed to recognize my symptoms, tell someone, and then reach out for professional help. This was not one of those things I could do on my own.

If you're reading this and think you can do it on your own, I'd like to lovingly say that eventually, you will need support of some kind, especially if you are in any type of recovery, fleeing domestic abuse, starting over. These things require you to use different coping skills, relational skills, esteem building skills that you might not have had experience with. It never hurts to gather wisdom and learn a new skill from someone who has some experience with what you are going through. And it definitely doesn't hurt to have *more* support than you have now.

We were made to be in community with one another. Our babies cry to be held, consoled, and cared for. When you're healing from trauma or any other mental illness or emotional event, it takes others to come alongside you to help you feel safe, loved, and important. Your recovery and your healing are important. They set the tone for the rest of your life moving forward. They provide the foundation for bigger and better future decisions and rewards. For an increased sense of safety, peace, and security. Making the decision to open up for help allows you to enjoy friendships with those who get to see you blossom and be your true self.

I remember the day I realized that the self I always knew was within me had remained unchanged after all the trauma and turmoil of the preceding years. Except on that day, I realized I was free to live an authentic life apart from oppression and abuse. What an amazing realization that was! I felt so light, and because I opened myself up to allow help and community in. I had people to celebrate that freedom with.

But I have no friends. May I suggest you take an inventory to discover what it is you want from life, and what misconceptions, faulty thinking, or fears you may have about the idea of community? You don't have to have all the friends or all the supports you need *right now*. You can start with one. You can search out blogs that discuss the topic you're struggling with, contact national hotlines, regional emergency numbers, and go online for resource lists in your area. There are therapy offices that work on an income-based sliding fee scale. There are all kinds of therapists specialized in nearly every area of practice: trauma, PTSD, marriage, faith-based, substance abuse/treatment, OCD, foster care, anxiety, depression, postpartum care, mom issues, dad issues, parenting issues, spending issues, eating issues and self-harm behaviors, sex therapy … there are even faith-based sex therapists! I mean, if you can name it, chances are there's a therapist out there that can see you about it. If you start with a therapist, the two of you can work together to address your lack of other social supports and healthy and positive relationships in order to increase those networks in your life.

All of this may feel insurmountable. Asking for help in a culture that makes a person feel inadequate, defective, and less than for experiencing real human issues is hard. Remember that there are pros and cons to our connected society. Living in the digital age of online community can be great! It can help connect people in ways they never would have been able to ten or fifteen years ago. But all that connectedness can also make you feel even more of an isolated anomaly. People do not want to feel inadequate in any way. Our culture has raised us to believe that we need to stand out for all the great things we can be, have, and do. Social media posts are flooded with best-case scenarios, our society applauds and makes richer those who are physically attractive with their symmetrical features and big bank accounts. Naturally, others try to emulate their looks and lifestyle, only to realize that the House of Social Media is built of cards and is an illusion.

Reality is messy, complicated, and dare I say it?—Ugly. It consists of infidelity and divorce. It is teenagers who struggle in dark places with dark thoughts. It is a stark contrast to the facade of well-manicured hands, lawns, children, and lives. Most things on social media are not an accurate depiction of the humanity that exists despite our best selfies. Yet, there is a double standard in regard to social media. When people project too much good, they are judged as being conceited, egotistical, boastful, and attention-seeking. When people are more authentic, they are judged as being dramatic, emotional, disturbed, and again, attention-seeking. Even as I write this book, I was told that I'm only writing it for attention. You know what? That person was absolutely correct. Their words were meant as a slight, but I can tell you that I absolutely want to bring attention to the devastating effects suffering alone has on the person who feels they have no one to reach out to for help. I want others to know it's okay to be yourself, to be vulnerable, to open up, and to talk to someone. And it is absolutely one million percent okay to not feel pressured to fit into someone else's idea of 'normal', successful, or happy. Please do not try to live up to someone else's standards or compare yourself to others. Your healing journey encompasses one day at a time. One healthy decision at a time.

With all the opportunities to gather your supports, your people, there is still something to be said for using wisdom in choosing who to open up to. Moving to a new area, I had to meet new people and develop a new network of friends. I had a friend whom I became close to. My kids loved her, and over the course of a few years, I had shared a bit about a few of my life experiences as they related to whatever conversation we were having. And she shared hers. The last night we saw one another, she explained that she doesn't understand how I have been able to make it through my life experiences without "going crazy." She had to distance herself from another friend because this other person was disorganized, made poor and even dangerous decisions, and demanded more of their friendship than my friend was comfortably able to give. But she compared me to this person, and followed up with, "I guess, I'm just waiting for the other shoe to fall." I had to ask her if she was concerned with me being around her children, and though she denied it, she hasn't really engaged with me since. She simply could not understand how I could come out of so many traumatic, and chaotic experiences while also leading a healthy and fulfilling life. She was waiting for me to snap, become unstable, or maybe even dangerous and decided she needed to pull away from our friendship.

Of course, this incident stung, but not for long. I am sharing this encounter with you because there are times you may find yourself in this exact situation. It just means that that person or group of people are not your people. Not everyone will understand you and what you've experienced, but you will be okay. You *will* find those who have the capacity to love or engage you in deep and meaningful relationships and friendships without demanding perfection. It is sad, but people most commonly judge others based on how they see themselves. What my friend was communicating is that she didn't feel *she* could make it through what I shared with her without having a breakdown. She may have thought she couldn't trust her own stability if she went through my experiences, so she couldn't trust mine.

It's encounters like these that enable us to discover what we value most in our relationships with others, and what we believe in. I know that God has done a complete healing in my heart and mind, and by his grace and mercy, the essence of who He created me to be has remained throughout these experiences. I have attended years of therapy, and fought hard to heal, and to forgive, and to move forward with passion and purpose. It is not my responsibility, nor yours, to prove any of that to others. You are only responsible and in control of your own thoughts, decisions, and behaviors. You cannot be responsible for how others perceive you. Please read that again. So, you keep going and searching for your people. You *will* find them! Please do not be discouraged by the few. Your life story will connect with others who need to know how you made it, and they will find you incredibly strong, rather than weak. They will value you and your friendship, instead of discarding it. Make sure you find those people, and don't worry about the rest.

In closing, I want you to know that you have many options for building your support networks. I hope you can learn how to recognize healthy behaviors in yourself and others, and set healthy boundaries (more on that later). Your story matters, and so do you. You will find your people. You will find and develop friendships that are healthy and life-giving. You will find people that you can be your true authentic self with, who can hold you accountable, and hold you up in prayer. These are the kinds of friends and supports that will stick with you through healthy conflict resolution, and who will be able to communicate in loving ways their need to part should that time come. I'm going to borrow a quote from one of my favorite books growing up, *Anne of Green Gables* by L.M. Montgomery: "Kindred spirits are not so scarce as I used to think. It's splendid to find out there are so many of them in the world." [12] Those are the keepers. Those are your village.

- What characteristics do you value most when it comes to friendships and community?

- Who would you consider part of your village community? Please list friends, family, neighbors, community members, etc. below.

- If you lack a supportive community, where are some places for you to start looking for one? List some local, national, or online support groups below.

- List two one-week, one-month, and six-month goals for gathering a community around you or digging deeper in the community you already have.

    One Week:

    One Month:

    Six Months:

CHAPTER FIVE

A Darkness Within

"Every person sees the world through their own heart, a viewfinder that colors their perceptions and molds the mental script that they incessantly replay in their mind." [13]

- KILROY J. OLDSTER

"He doesn't wait until I'm awake. He comes into my unconscious to find me, to pull me out. He seizes my logical mind and disables it with fear. I awake already panic-stricken, afraid I won't answer the voice correctly, the loud, clear voice that reverberates in my head like an alarm that can't be turned off.

What did you eat last night?

Since we first met when I was twelve, he's been with me, at me, barking orders. A drill sergeant of a voice that is pushing me forward, marching ahead, keeping time. When the voice isn't giving orders, it's counting. Like a metronome, it is predictable. I can hear the tick of another missed beat and in the silence between beats I anxiously await *the next tick; like the constant noise of an intermittently dripping faucet, it keeps counting in the silences when I want to be still. It tells me to never miss a beat. It tells me I will get fat again if I do." (de Rossi, 3)* [14]

Wow. Impactful.

My husband always tells me I have the mind of an engineer, and truth be told my biological father is an engineer, so I'd like to believe that it's in me too. But I think I chose counseling as a profession because human brains are the most complicated machines on earth. So, when a friend of mine recommended this book, it was because she knew my love of the inner workings of one's mind. I didn't know what to expect when I picked up *Unbearable Lightness*. I wasn't expecting to read such an honest and upfront account of something that I think most people struggle with but never discuss. The author describes her inner voice as if it were a male drill sergeant. And since I am a very visual person, I imagine him to be about six-foot-four with scars and a permanent scowl fixed angrily on his reddened, and leathery worn face. She does an amazing job providing us a window into a room in her mind that most of us are very familiar with; except in our room the occupant differs.

If I had to describe my inner voice, it would probably resemble a cast consisting of different versions of me from different points in my life. There's the frightened and hypervigilant girl who sometimes makes an appearance when I am at my most sleep-deprived. She is the one always trying to put up walls to protect me from any hint of danger. I have had to work alongside her with compassion and patience to let her know that we're safe. We're okay. There's the angsty teenager who is angry at the world for all the things she couldn't control about our past. She lashes out at everyone within a ten-foot radius when she feels most vulnerable. But I value her because she doesn't take crap from anyone and she has given me the strength I need to stand up for myself in oppressing situations. And though she isn't a mother, her grit and energy give me what I need to protect my children. There's the calm and laid-back woman who assures me everything will be okay and encourages me in my faith. I imagine her sitting in a field with her eyes closed, face turned towards the sunlight. She always has a scripture verse to whisper to me on the hardest days and lets me know it's okay to nap, or stop and reflect on where God has brought me. There's the anxious girl who isn't quite sure I can handle the world and makes me question everything. Her anxiety annoys me at times, but I'm thankful for her because she has kept me from making some pretty bad decisions in hindsight. There's the brave and confident woman who charges ahead and gets things done (I swear she's connected to a caffeine drip), but that woman has *definitely* gotten us in way over our head at times and scrambling to think on our feet to find a way out. All these voices tug and pull and vie for my attention. But the one that bullies them all is the slimy, yellowed creature that constantly berates me and tells me what a fake I am. This voice tells me that I am unloved, unclean, and unworthy of anything and everything that would resemble peace, or trust, or love. I can't even call this thing a person, because it is a creature that has held onto every trauma, every heartache, every abuse, and every derogatory word ever spoken against me. This thing is the DVR of my life that I didn't subscribe to, and my life experiences have disfigured its body beyond all recognition. And its gravelly voice is the one I wrestle against even now as I write this book.

When you take a moment to look back on your life, have you ever stopped to think about who occupies the room that holds your inner voice? I'm not talking about the voice that provides you with a running commentary on everything from daily to-do lists, worries about your children and family, and which character from your favorite tv show is next to exit in dramatic fashion. I'm talking about the voice, or voices, that run in the background of all that day-to-day din. For me, one of these voices always sounded like the scene from *Friends* where Ross tries to pull up his leather pants—frantic, critical, scrambling for a solution, disappointed—without the laughter. Instead, I'm just left with paste pants, hiding in a bathroom with no way out, running through all the scenarios I should have tried but didn't and embarrassed that I failed … again. That would be the girl that always worries I can't do something, and is quick to say, "I told you so!"

I never gave much thought to this inner running dialogue—with all the mixed voices—until recent years. Where did these voices come from? How did they develop? I could probably pinpoint the start of these voices as a child in foster care. I was at a friend's house and asked for a drink because I was thirsty. It was an innocent enough question, but my foster brother was in the kitchen at this friend's house too. He looked at me and said, "You're always *begging* for something!" And everyone in the house, including my friend's parents, laughed. That was the first time I was publicly humiliated for asking for help; a simple and innocent question. This was also the first time I had a critical remark made that implied so many things about my character and motives at the time, and was the start of my need to please others and present myself as a self-sufficient person. It didn't take long for that remark to expand in my mind to thoughts and feelings of inadequacy. This incident added to the slime sticking to that oppressive creature, who is always at the ready to remind me of this memory and many like it at a moment's notice.

    Over the years, this voice became increasingly demanding of perfection and hard work in every single area of my life. I also felt the rejection of my mother and knew that I wanted to focus on living life in a way that was completely opposite of how she lived hers. I took in feedback from peers, from family members, teachers, sports instructors, and compared them to my developing inner dialogue, mine and society's ideals, and the goals I had for myself. All those things combined to form my collective inner-voice. I began acting on those more positive voices from the people that showed me care and attention, who encouraged me to see my own value and worth.

In time, I discovered a greater voice impressed upon my heart and mind—the voice of God. Obviously, his voice wasn't auditory but 'heard' through his word, and through the people around me. His word described me as a daughter. He reminded me with every sunset, birdsong, and blade of grass just how loved I am. His voice never hid, never backed down, and never condemned me for the decisions I made. He continues to love, support, and convict by His Holy Spirit. I believe it is He who preserved me through all of my experiences, and healed me so I can come alongside others in their healing journey. And I will be eternally grateful for the ability to hear His voice and read His word.

One of my favorite things about books, movies, and plays is that they allow you to connect with and examine humanity from a safe distance, including your own. I illustrated this at the beginning of this chapter, when I included a passage from *Unbearable Lightness: A Story of Loss and Gain*. Portia de Rossi showed bravery by sharing so much of her inner thought life with the world. In doing so she positioned herself as *one of us* in a way that is relatable and real. Quite a few characters in cinematic history have had to struggle with their inner voice in different ways. Let's take the character Darth Vader. If you are not familiar, this tyrant of a man began life as Anakin Skywalker. He lost his mother, was enslaved as a child, and over time, developed a fear of the darkness and power he possessed. He feared the darkness would destroy his family, and the person he loved most in the world. When his wife died because of events he enacted, he fully turned to the dark side. He fell prey to the inner voice that wished to destroy him, and he became Darth Vader. He was filled with so much hatred, and rage that he could not see himself clearly. He could not believe any good existed in him. He became a beacon of death and destruction, and sought revenge by placing blame on a group of people that was not the cause of his fear, or his wife's death. Ultimately, this turning led to his own destruction, only realizing much too late that he did indeed possess good in his heart.

Darth Vader surrounded himself by people that only encouraged and validated the darkness of his inner voice within. He allowed his fear, anger, rage, and unforgiveness to overcome him. And he stayed there, without anyone to help lift him up out of that. The only person that could have made any impact on his heart and mind had died. He was lost. But you don't have to be. You can choose forgiveness for yourself and others. You can choose to surround yourself with people who believe in the goodness you possess. You do not have to continue in self-destructive ways. You can live! You can grow! You can learn! And apply what you learn today to tomorrow.

By comparison, Moana was a girl who was raised to fulfill a single role—to become the chieftess of her people. Her parents taught her the path she was expected to follow, but there was yet another voice that encouraged her to listen to who she knew she was. The voice of Moana's grandmother always came to her when she needed her the most. She reminded her of who she was when she felt most lost and ready to give up her quest. Moana, in turn, took her grandmother's wisdom and shared it with the great monster, Te Ka, at the end of the movie. Moana explains that she journeyed across the ocean to find Te Ka, and sings "they have stolen the heart from inside you/ But this does not define you/ This is not who you are/ You know who you are (echoing what her own grandmother instilled in her)." At the sound of these words, Te Ka transforms from the lava-spewing monster whose anger spread across the globe blighting everything it touched, into the life-giving Goddess Te Fiti, who restores everything she touches.

The movie *Moana* does a great job of illustrating the importance of change agents in your life. Change agents are those around you who help to encourage and facilitate healthy and positive change. I can point to many different change agents along my own path. They were men and women who saw me, without judgement, and listened to me, validated my concerns, and did not dismiss my traumatic experiences. They saw my potential and reflected it back to me on a daily basis until I began to see it for myself. Moana's change agent was her grandmother, always speaking truth and wisdom into her life. And in turn, Moana was Te Ka's change agent, who spoke the truth and helped Te Ka to feel seen and heard. Moana was not afraid of the hardened exterior that was a result of the pain and trauma that Te Ka felt and experienced. These change agents helped to combat the dark thoughts and reinforce healing thoughts and practices. They each lent strength, courage, and love to the other and created a safe space for healing to happen.

I don't want you to go over to the dark side, like Darth Vader, and surround yourself with those who would only encourage you to continue harming yourself and others in thought, word, and deed because of your own pain. If you're already there, then please know that you are worthy of change. Change is possible for you. Seek out for yourself healthy change agents who can provide a safe place for you to expose and question your inner dialogue, and help you find ways to stop the cycle of abuse towards yourself. Living a life of peace and restoration is so worth the struggle it can be to confront the source of your own negative self-talk and cling to the hope that your future days do not have to be the same as your bitter yesterdays.

- What are some repeated themes to your inner thoughts?

- Where did some of these messages come from?

- Who would you consider to be positive and healthy role models/ change agents along the way? These people can be someone in your own circle, or even literary, fictional, etc.

- Do you believe changing the way you think about and toward yourself is possible? If so, why? If not, why?

CHAPTER SIX:

The Blind Side

"A shadow is never created in darkness. It is born of light. We can be blind to it and blinded by it. Our shadow asks us to look at what we don't want to see." [15]

- TERRY TEMPEST WILLIAMS

"I'm okay. I'm fine. Everything is good. I'm good." Sound familiar? This is a mantra we like to repeat to ourselves when there are things about our lives, our circumstances, our emotional and mental pain that we don't want to see, feel, or discuss with anyone. It's like coming up alongside a sailing vessel adrift at sea. The captain is sitting at the bow with his eyes on the horizon yet does not see the storm above him. He does not see his boat taking on water, nor does he try to bail himself out, as he believes he is still anchored within the safety of the harbor. He sits in the storm, oblivious to the tragedy about to befall him. All the while, you are there beside him waving wildly, unable to get into his boat because of the surge of ocean waves. So, all you can do is watch as he slowly goes under. The real tragedy here? You are both the captain *and* the person trying to alert him to his situation in vain.

That's kind of what it's like to have a blind spot and not realize it. Blind spots beg to be discovered. We embark on the journey of discovering what we don't know we don't know about ourselves, and our hidden mental, emotional, and psychological pain. It is a master at hiding, and has ways of remaining hidden for years. Conversely, physical pain is almost always brought to the forefront of our minds so we can react and seek healing. The former pain shows up in odd ways, like suddenly forgetting how to get to work, like gaining or losing weight with no underlying medical conditions, like constantly over-drafting bank accounts without any recollection as to why.

Hidden mental and emotional pain *don't want* to be found. And your heart and mind don't want to go looking for its source either. Our hidden pain and ways of coping sway together as two partners in a mesmerizing ballad, each holding the other up. At first, this dance begins as a gentle sway to lull us away from the trauma and help us feel safe. Then, slowly, it spins into a frantic dance that depletes our energy and leaves us trapped on the dancefloor without realizing how we got there. We find ourselves moving to a beat that isn't our own, and fear that by discovering the source of the chaos we're caught in the music will abruptly end. We'll be forced to stop and take a look at ourselves and face the pain. After all, unless the cancer is revealed, it cannot be removed. So, we must have the courage to look within. And in looking, we have a great opportunity to find what it is that is eating us away. We can seek healing. And by healing, we can return to the peaceful rhythms of life again.

Now, not knowing what we don't know and willfully ignoring the things we do are two completely different beasts. I was a young nineteen-year-old home for my winter break from college when I began dating my ex-husband, a person I met on the school bus my senior year of high school. Because I had not gained the wisdom that only comes with time and experience, I eventually married this person. I described this time in my life earlier in the book. But at the time, all I cared about was that he was funny, attractive, and made me feel cared about. I spent the next almost nine years willfully ignoring a host of behaviors that were major red flags, and betrayals that cut deep. Suffice it to say I knew all about the things I was ignoring, and their consequences, but I continued to willfully ignore them anyways. Why? Well, after some reflection I can say that I was holding onto two different people: the person I thought he was when we met, and the person I always thought he could be. I scoff at myself now as I write those words because of how foolish I was. Neither of those people were real. They were like trying to hold onto smoke with my bare hands.

How often have you ignored the signs and symptoms of a sinking ship that are right in front of you? Throughout my marriage, I was like the captain above who ignores what's in front of him in favor of looking out to the horizon, waiting for some change to come without addressing the immediate danger. But we don't just do this in relationships, as in my case. This can occur in any circumstance where the pain feels too overwhelming to confront head-on. When I was a young girl, I used to love climbing trees and swinging from vines. On any given day, you could find my brother and I in the woods across the street from our house exploring. Now, the children in our neighborhood excluded my brother and I from a clubhouse they were building so we begged our father to help us build one. One day, I was swinging across a ravine on a vine and I looked across and saw my dad and brother on the other side. In my dad's hand was an axe. Immediately, I became overly excited. This could only mean one thing: he was ready to chop down some small trees to help us build our own clubhouse fort. In my excitement, I jumped off the vine onto a foam cushion at the bottom of the ravine. Instead of propelling me up to my father as my ten-year-old mind reasoned, the cushion swallowed my foot causing me to fall and gash my kneecap wide open. Since my father was already there, he ran down the ravine, scooped me up and took me home to wash out my wound, assess the damage, and determine the best course of action—go to the hospital. It was there that they washed out my wound some more and gave me some stitches, medicine, and specific instructions for care that I had to follow exactly so I could regain proper movement of my knee without pain. If I did not want to risk permanent disability and pain to this crucial joint made for mobility, I needed to heed the care instructions carefully.

Most of our physical wounds follow this course of action: clean out, assess damage, and decide on home or professional care. We're given a prescription for exact care instructions, which usually includes a time of rest or covering over the affected area to give it time and space to heal. Sure, sometimes there's plenty of pain along that process to recovery but the pain serves a purpose and helps us to gauge the healing process. What would not have been healthy for me to do would be to ignore the bleeding wound, continue swinging on the vine, or climbing trees as if the wound didn't exist, all the while my condition would worsen. Yet, that's what we do with psychological and emotional pain. All. The. Time. How amazing would it be if we treated our psychological and emotional wounds with the same care and attention we do our physical wounds?

More importance is placed on an arm or a leg because they enable us to move throughout our world and engage with others in physical ways. But our physical selves are not the only part that makes us who we are. It is about time our culture, and society — including you — begin to recognize the importance of our psychological, emotional, and spiritual health and wellbeing. These other parts help us to connect with others in meaningful and life-giving ways. These other parts allow us the time to pause and reflect on everything around us. These other parts house the *essence* of our beings, and so often these are the parts of ourselves that are *neglected* or *ignored* the most! Especially when fear of confronting the pain is involved.

Oftentimes, pain in these other areas of our being manifest in different ways. Now we're getting into the area of discovering what we don't know we don't know. When we experience this intangible pain, there is a tendency to cope with it in many ways. We have come up with all ways and manners of coping with this pain. The creative ways we have devised to cope and assuage the pain can and often do lead to devastating consequences. When people think of addiction, they might immediately think of illicit substances, alcohol, or prescription medication. If they have been exposed to other forms of addiction or addictive behaviors their list might even include things like gambling, and pornography or sex. I include these things in this chapter because unhealthy ways of coping begin innocently enough, but snowball out of control. Over time they often increase the pain they were meant to cover in intense and varied ways. But the list of unhealthy coping for psychological or emotional pain doesn't end with substances, gambling, or illicit images. Unhealthy coping is anything that draws your time, attention, energy, resources, and focus away from your mental, emotional, and psychological pain in a way that prevents or hinders the healing process. Read that again, aloud, for the people in the back! Some people notice they can't stop buying things for themselves, their homes, children, grandchildren, or others. Some allow themselves to be immersed in fantasy by games, books, television, or endless planning for their future through apps like Pinterest (yep, I went there) while tuning out the rest of the world, and their psychological and emotional pain right with it. Still, others invest all their time and energy in their paid or volunteer work with little to no rest, their image or perception without connection with others, controlling as many aspects of their children's lives as they can, and even the legalistic aspects of their own faiths or religions. These can all be warning signs that there may be some underlying issues, or pain, that need attention.

So, why would someone willfully or unknowingly ignore their pain? For me, and many others, fear was at the top of my list of reasons why I didn't face my own pain. Actually, fear could probably be considered the only reason. Fear of the unknown is so powerful. It has crippled nations and destroyed lives. A client of mine in substance abuse treatment said one of the most profound things I have ever heard in session. This statement came after months of resistance before finally surrendering to the therapeutic process. They said, "Knowing about yourself sucks because then you have to do something about it." Some have spent their entire lives, and sometimes fortunes, to build a life that reflects the exact opposite of the pain they have endured as children and young adults. Some fear that without the image they built as protection, they would be forced to face the pain of their experiences, the pain of what their true selves might actually be, or the pain of disappointment at a seemingly unchanging outward situation. But facing that pain doesn't have to be done alone, nor does it have to be a mortally wounding process in and of itself. When you are walking alongside a caring and compassionate therapist, friend or mentor, this person can help you explore and examine the pain from a safe distance. You can heal from it bit by bit until one day you realize the memories of the pain do not affect you at all. Huzzah! But as long as you continue to allow it to hide deep within your heart, mind, soul, and psyche it can have power over you. By fully engaging in the healing process, you take that power back!

So how can you tell if you're missing something you can't see? It takes courage to make the decision to stop ignoring the pain, and turn a listening ear towards it. I said before that my husband tells me I have the mind of an engineer. He is a systems engineer, but when I think of the mind, I think of a great big machine. I am not as mechanically inclined as my husband or our friend Craig. He is a mechanical engineer, so I turn to him for random things like doing research for this particular chapter. He had no idea what this chapter was about, but was willing to try to answer my questions as best as he could. I asked, "What are some typical signs of breakdown of a machine when something is wrong or needs attention that someone who works regularly with the machine might miss?" He asked me to clarify if I meant signs even a seasoned mechanic could miss, to which I replied, yes. He responded by explaining that "a seasoned mechanic is the one who should be able to identify and recognize the symptoms that could indicate larger problems down the road. But to attempt to answer the question ... [by] listening to the machine. Changes in the overall tone of a machine, listening for squeaks, hums, or vibration changes, can easily be missed. If your mind's eye can't remember what the machine used to sound like, you may not recognize that change in sound." Thank you, Craig! He didn't realize it at the time, of course, just how helpful his explanation was. You see, it helps for us to know who we are or who we were before the inflicted pain, trauma, or loss. We have to be willing to listen through the pain for all the changes it created deep within us. Pain, trauma, grief ... it all leaves a trail that we can follow back to find the person we were stuck standing there at its source. Through sharing our experiences, engaging in the therapeutic process, gathering our positive support system, and replacing unhealthy thoughts and behaviors with healthy forms of coping, we can reach a loving hand across to help ourselves heal from that pain. We have to be willing to listen carefully and respond bravely.

Healing isn't easy. It takes time and intention. We have to be willing to look at ourselves and our situations with the courage it takes to challenge any unhealthy thoughts, and behaviors we discover so we can experience the peace, and joy that comes with healing. Listen, there is no way you can live long enough to do everything on your Pinterest boards. Nor can you correct or change events or decisions you've already made. But what you can do is put your phone down, and be more present with yourself, your spouses, children, family, and friends. You can choose to live your life today completely present and open to its possibilities—all of them. Even the painful ones that produce healing and perseverance. One of the greatest disservices our culture has done is to make us believe that the best life we can live is a life free of all manners of pain. Entire industries have been created around this idea, and gladly market to us ways that numb, distract, or erase any kind of pain we might have the opportunity to encounter. But there are better, more kind, more present, and more nourishing ways to move along with and through the pain that enable you to draw closer to the healthy and whole person you want to be. You just need to take the time to listen, discover, uncover, and heal.

- Make a list of five positive attributes and qualities you like about yourself.

- What are some criticisms you've received recently? Is there any truth to these criticisms?

- What are things you hesitate to confront about yourself, your life, circumstances, or relationships? And how do you respond to someone bringing light to one of these areas?

- Do you find yourself using unhealthy coping to deal with feelings of psychological or emotional discomfort? If so, what do you think they are? Be totally honest with yourself. This is a safe space. (If you're journaling, you can just write keywords down for yourself that only you understand.)

- What are ways that you check in with yourself, or listen for signs that things need addressed? Do you think you'd be willing to get help with what you've found?

CHAPTER SEVEN:

Moving Forward with Purpose

"In the long run, we shape our lives, and we shape ourselves. The process never ends until we die. And the choices we make are ultimately our own responsibility." [16]

- ELEANOR ROOSEVELT

I know that chapter was a bit much to take in. It asked a lot of you back there. I mean, I asked you to look behind the curtain and see the things you don't really want to know or look at. If you've done that in any sort of capacity, I want to take a moment now to tell you how proud I am of you. This healing process isn't easy and looks differently for each of us. For some, it takes rigorous honesty and accountability. For others, it takes bravery, patience, and grace. It takes having people around you to lift you up when you think you can't stand up against the weight of your past, your trauma, your mistakes, and everything that goes along with it. But you did it. *You* did. No one else.

Now what? Now, my friend, you have to make a decision on how you want to proceed with your life. I know that sounds scary and complicated, but it doesn't have to be. You can just take one small step at a time. And promise you will continue to check in with yourself, and continue to take a look at all those things you'd rather not look at. Like I said previously, "Knowing about yourself sucks, because then you have to do something about it." Once you know, *you can't unknow*. If you're sitting here reading this and thinking to yourself, *I have known about these things for years but I'm still not ready to make a decision about them*. Or you're thinking, *It's not that easy. I have nowhere to go. I have kids. I can't just uproot our whole lives*. I hear you. And for you I say, breathe. It will be okay. I'm not here to *make* anyone do anything. I just want to encourage you to keep taking steps forward, no matter how small.

When I think about moving forward, I think about my divorces. Yes, divorces, plural. I have had two of them, as you've read. Each marriage and divorce brought trauma and heartache. Moving forward with my life from these experiences took hard work. It took humility and to accept that I needed help. But first I needed to get over my guilt and shame. And sometimes people around you won't make that easy. I once had a pastor who knew my soon-to-be ex-husband and I approach me at my place of employment and tell me in front of my coworkers so they could hear him say, "Jackie, you need to stop this cycle of divorce." My jaw dropped, and so did theirs. I was in the middle of my job, just days after fleeing an unhealthy situation. This man believed the stories he was told, and blamed *me* for exiting my marriage. I closed my eyes and took a deep breath. I pulled him aside and asked him not to address my private life at my workplace again. As a man belonging to the church, as well as someone connected to the profession of counseling, he violated all kinds of ethics. But from that moment on, I decided that I was no longer going to allow someone else to shame me for the decisions I made. I wasn't going to allow myself to feel shame, either. I can be remorseful for the decisions I've made. I can regret these same decisions, but there is no way am I going to feel ashamed. This is my life and I have to take ownership of every decision I make. And I will do so unashamed.

When you make the decision to move forward without shame, you find yourself free to move forward with purpose. The question then becomes how do you find your purpose? Each time I have had to start over, or to heal, I have had to reflect on my purpose in embarking on the journey towards healing. As in the case of fleeing the unhealthy situation above, my purpose was to find and maintain safety and begin the process of healing and discovery. There were things I needed to leave behind; things like worrying about what people thought about me and my situation, worrying about where I would live, worrying about what was being said about me by my ex. Because the truth was that there are two people on this earth that know the truth about some of these situations, and I'm one of them. I knew the truth, and I knew that I found safety out of that situation. As for the other things, I trusted that God would take care of the rest and provide my needs. And thankfully, he did. For me, I sought healing through my faith in God, prayer, being in a community of supportive people, and processing through trauma, betrayal, unforgiveness, abandonment, etc. with a caring and compassionate therapist. I sought and found purpose in healing by this same pathway.

As difficult as each small step forward was to take, I felt an internal motivation to dig deeper into my own mental and emotional pain and discomfort. I felt my purpose was to continue to fight anxiety, PTSD, and depression so I could help light the way for others who would soon be fighting their way out of their own darkness.

As for change, I was ready and committed to making changes that brought me out of my comfort zone, but it took some pretty serious situations to get to that point. For years, I struggled back and forth through some stages of change. The changes I really needed to make for myself went beyond culturally acceptable changes like dietary shifts or social media fasts. The changes I needed to make were related to how I was going to choose to see myself, the world, my past, and my future. And I needed to make a decision to see those things differently each and every day, until they became part of my daily life. Those kinds of changes can take years to achieve and maintain, and I went through several stages of change on my way to moving forward with purpose. I had to come to the point of engaging in the change process. No one could do it for me. While embarking on my healing journey, I found the model of behavior change developed by Prochaska and DiClemente [17] to be helpful in being able to gauge my readiness to get started. This is probably the 'most' therapist-like section of this entire half of the book, but I hope you find the information to be helpful. The model isn't perfect, and was originally intended to be used with people who were battling addictive behaviors related to nicotine use. While some people have added stages, these five are generally the most agreed upon ones, with a sixth stage that most people might not use. I'll provide a brief explanation of the model and its stages below:

- **Pre-contemplation**

    Before your eyes landed on this book you were probably unaware of the ways in which your trauma, negative experiences, or ways of coping were affecting your mental, emotional, psychological, and physical health, your familial or romantic relationships, friendships, finances, employment or ability to care for your own needs. This stage is about raising your internal awareness of how your life experiences and the way you cope with them not only affect you in all the aforementioned areas, but how they affect others and the environment around you. Remember what we talked about in the last chapter? This stage is filled with the things you don't know that you don't know, but it's also here that you begin to find out.

- **Contemplation**

    So now you're at the place in your life that you realize that some of the behaviors you're engaging in might have served a purpose for you initially (like shutting out the world when you felt too stressed or depressed to deal, taking something for the pain, responding to people in harsh ways, etc.) but now that your life is changing, and evolving, these behaviors don't necessarily match the stage of life you're in *right now*. So, you begin to reflect on your behavior in ways that bring you to question them. Is there a better way to react, to deal, to engage others? Probably. You begin to go through the process of weighing the pros and cons of making a change. How much effort will it take on your part? Do you have the energy, time, resources, and supports in place to start employing the changes you want and need to make?

- **Preparation**

    You've shifted from being unaware to becoming aware of how your behaviors are affecting you, and people or environments around you. You've even begun to think about what your life would look like with these new changes in them. You have made time to seek out some support for yourself. You might have already begun telling people you are about to make some new changes. You might have approached others to begin mending your relationship, apologizing for the pain you've caused them. You also might have begun to test the waters of change and though you haven't achieved consistency, the small changes you've made feel good. You really start to believe that change is not only possible, but achievable, and you feel the beginnings of hope. The hope you feel empowers you to commit fully to your new changes.

- **Action**

    You've gained the confidence to enact your positive changes more consistently and are really beginning to experience the rewards of choosing to live life differently than you had before. You have enlisted the help of people you trust, and they have become your sounding board. You can turn to them when you've reacted, behaved, or chosen differently than you would have liked. You are replacing negative behaviors and thinking of ways to help yourself continue healthy ways of living.

- **Maintenance**

   Some time has passed, and your positive changes are like second nature now. But you still may be tempted to return to old behaviors. Your positive support system has now helped to keep you accountable. You can be honest about your thoughts and feelings towards certain temptations that would pull you towards unhealthy behaviors. You've begun to develop some relapse prevention tools to help you maintain the positive change(s) you worked so hard for.

- **Termination**

   Now this last stage is the one that is left out of most lists when describing this particular model for change. Termination is when you've wholeheartedly decided and believe that you are in no way going to return to the unhealthy coping, decisions, or behaviors of the past. You have considered those things to be terminated in your life. The reason most lists leave off this last stage is because it is generally believed that most people will be in maintenance for most of their lives; always engaging in relapse prevention and never fully rid of the temptation to turn back. But I thought I'd include this stage, so you have a better understanding of where most people start and where they'd like to end up in regard to making changes for themselves.

So how do you feel about those stages? Where do you see yourself in there in regards to things you want to change? I mean, let's be honest here. Not a single one of us is perfect. There are things I have definitely reached termination with, but still, other behaviors that I'm in contemplation about. Do I really want to change in those other areas? Yeah, I'm still working that all out. But the point is to be honest and open with yourself so you can discover areas of your life that aren't serving you or others well. Then you have the opportunity to decide what to do with what you've come across during your time of self-reflection. I get it. Change is so hard. Often it feels like a huge, overwhelming, and insurmountable task. You may be like me, and struggle with Imposter Syndrome. What's is that, you ask? Let me tell you. It's the feeling that *maybe* you aren't really as (fill in the blank) as you think you are, and you're just pretending to be those things. And the fear that one day, *everyone* else will discover this about you, too. But that's all the more reason to make time to reflect on how your thoughts, behaviors, decisions, and reactions are affecting and serving you *now* at this stage of life. After all, you may just discover that you are stronger and smarter than you thought. Besides that, you may also come to find that you are just the person you think you are, with the potential to do above and beyond what you thought possible. You can do this. You *can* change. You can break the cycle of addiction and every unhealthy thing in your family, or your own life. You can be the change agent for future generations. You.

So, what is your purpose in this life? How do you feel about making changes? Is this a scary and daunting thing for you or do you feel hopeful for the potential that lies under the surface of these thoughts? You aren't alone. There are many people rooting for you, and if you believe, there's a God that can lead you into you the life he has for you. A life filled with peace, and connectedness, and joy. George Addair was quoted as saying, "Everything you've ever wanted is on the other side of fear." [18] It's a quote I have turned to often in my own personal life. Don't let fear hold you back from making positive changes towards healing and healthy relationships. You have lived so many years through the worst things you have ever been through without an advocate for yourself. Now you have the opportunity to be the person who advocates for change within yourself. I hope you grab a hold of this opportunity with everything you have, because you're worth it. You are loved and cared for. You matter. Your life matters. Your life has purpose and meaning. You just need to take time to discover what that is.

By now you should come to expect these questions. Grab your notebook or journal and let's begin:

- What behavior, situation, or decision is affecting your life in the most negative way, right now?

- What stage do you find yourself in, after reading the descriptions above?

- What is the purpose behind your desire to change?

- If you feel as though you don't need to change anything in your life, how can you support someone else in their decision to make changes?

CHAPTER EIGHT:

Eyes on the Prize

"It's okay to be scared. Being scared means you're about to do something really, really brave." [19]

- MANDY HALE

Confession time. I skipped this chapter while writing the book because by the time I got to this point in my writing journey, I just felt deflated and out of steam. Have you ever felt that way in your own life? Like you *just can't even* today. That was me and this chapter. So, I had to step away, skip over, work on something else and come back when I was ready. And you know what? It's totally okay to do while writing a book and living life. Your healing journey is completely unique to you. You could be rolling along and come across something in your path that causes you a moment, or month to pause. It's okay to put a pin there and hold the space to revisit when you're ready again. Don't worry. You will be ready to take a look at that thing, or feel that feeling, in time.

Lately, most of my inspiration has come from my experiences with my children because I spend the majority of my day caring for their needs. This has been the most humbling and illuminating time for me in my life. Motherhood has illuminated my unknown strengths and weaknesses, my fears and faith, the depth of my own selfishness, but also the ability to give more of myself than I thought possible. This role has really dismantled every part of myself that I held onto, and caused me to redefine my priorities, and things like personal space, comfort, a 'full night's rest', and 'free' time. I've had to lean so heavily on my faith in God and allow Him to strengthen me, because I cannot do this on my own.

Today was one of those days that I had to dig deep and find the strength to get the job done. My husband was away at a conference and I decided to take my children to a strawberry festival that was happening at a nearby orchard. This festival happens once a year, so of course there were no parking spots available and approximately five million people darting about, so I had to park off-site. But it worked out at the beginning of our adventure because we entered the farm at the exact spot we needed to be, at the top furthest most field. We were right there at the strawberry fields and were able to begin picking immediately. But then my son saw tractors pulling along passengers in their flatbeds, and he almost jumped in front of one of these machines in his rush to climb aboard. He was so patient as we picked berries that I thought there would be no harm in riding the tractor all the way down to the bottom of the hill to where most of the crowds were so he could play in the children's area.

He is very familiar with this place, as we visit at least once a week, but I have never taken the kids alone when it was so busy. When we got to the play area, my son was by my side. I had already prepared him for the crowds and made him promise he would stick close by. I nearly dropped the berries we picked and paid for and I turned my head for one moment, and when I turned back, he was gone. Out of sight. Children and families blocked every line of sight to every piece of play yard equipment and structure. I called his name, no reply. I called two, six, ten more times to no avail. At that point, I felt panic rise in my throat, and I reached for my cell phone to call my husband, holding back tears, I said, "I can't find our son! He's lost. I am screaming for an obviously lost child and people are just staring at me. No one is helping." A few more moments passed, probably less than five minutes total, and I looked up to see him wandering around in the next area where the cars were parked. He looked lost and was searching the crowd for me. I ran over to him and calmly explained that I had been searching for him, and that he needed to stay nearby. But because I did not want to lose sight of him again, I thought it better to just go back to the car and revisit this play area on a less crowded day.

This did not sit well with my young son, *at all*. He began to writhe and wail and try his best to pull away from my grasp to escape back into the throng of people I had just plucked him out of. I could not wait for another tractor to come and ride us up the huge hill, so what did I do? I removed my youngest from the carrier I had strapped to me, set her on the ground, and adjusted the straps to allow room for my still wailing and wiggling son. I placed him in the carrier, moved him to my back, picked up my bag, the kids' berries, and my daughter. She is half the size and weight of my son and so is much easier to carry in my arms than he is. Well, she saw the perfect opportunity to show her brother some solidarity, so she began to wail and wiggle too as I turned my face upward and began to climb the hill with my precious children. Carrying them up the hill was like trying to hold onto two jackhammers that had sirens attached to both ends. Each leaden step up that giant hill felt heavier than the previous, all my muscles and joints were screaming along with my two babes, and I had to stop frequently to catch my breath. It was nearly 80F / 27C, and the heat felt like a thousand suns beating down upon my brow. I tried to avoid eye contact with each passerby, but when our eyes happened to meet, I saw an understanding in their face that helped me to carry on towards my destination: home. Halfway up the hill, I felt like giving up. I was too far away from the bottom to catch a ride on a tractor, but I wasn't yet close enough to the top to see the area where the land leveled out. My children were each trying to topple out of my arms like a spilled bag of apples, and I felt ... exhausted, impatient, embarrassed, and wanted to be anywhere but where I was in that moment.

I didn't want to feel the pain in my lungs or legs. I didn't want to hear their cries anymore. But I chose instead to close my eyes, take a clearing breath and make a decision. I couldn't go back, and sitting down would not get me anywhere closer to my goals. It would just prolong the physical, mental, and emotional pain and discomfort I was in. I decided the best way forward was to keep going and to keep the end in my mind's eye. Along the way, I took time to hear the birds above the wails of my children, and appreciated the scene around me. The view from the hill on the rest of the orchard and farm below really was beautiful. It was nice to take time to notice families enjoying themselves and loving their children. Young couples were taking photos of themselves, and friends were laughing together as they hoisted each other up to help reach the cherries at the top of the trees. There is a popular endurance race around here called Tough Mudder. I even made myself laugh by telling myself, "Who needs Tough Mudder when I'm a tough mother?" I mean, that corny mom joke gave me a good chuckle that lasted until I reached the level ground at the top of the hill.

I was walking on an ankle injury that I have been in physical therapy for, and that was the first day I could pause to appreciate all the hard work I put in the last month. I recognized the mental and physical strength I possessed to complete the climb. And when we made it to the top, my children became calm because I was calm and they began to appreciate the scenery around me too, so much so, that my oldest asked to stop and have a picnic in the field. So, I set both kids down, pulled out their lunches, and we smiled, laughed and enjoyed each other's company. Even though I still had a bit of distance to go until I arrived at my destination, it was my shift in thinking and perspective that allowed me to enjoy and appreciate the journey. This appreciation provided me strength, and endurance, and peace in the midst of the chaos and pain.

Our healing journeys are like this, too. You may get to a place where you're beginning to make changes and feeling great about them, but aren't yet to the place where you've reached your goal. You start to experience some mental, emotional, or even physical discomfort in your progress because you've begun to pull away from old people, places, or ways of coping but haven't mastered the new healthy ways of living life. It's at this point that many people stop and contemplate going back. It's just easier, right? I mean, for me, I would have just had to walk back down the hill I was climbing. Surely, walking downhill would feel much better, right? But I knew the vehicle that would take me home was not in that direction, and going back would leave me stranded. I would have to walk up this hill, eventually. So, I chose to rest right where I was. I didn't go back, but I didn't go forward. Instead of giving up, I gave myself permission to pause in order to take inventory of how I was feeling and determine whether or not my energy stores were enough to complete the task. I readjusted my goals to find an intermediate stopping place just on the other side of the field, where I could rest again, and then use the last bit of energy I had to walk the last leg of my journey. For you, this could look like trying to get away from an unhealthy relationship. You've recognized your own value and worth and the unhealthy ways the relationship affected your mental, emotional, or even physical health. You've communicated your need to end the relationship. You're ready to make changes and may have begun putting protections in place for yourself to avoid contact with this person: blocked their number, informed your support system that your relationship is ending, begun filling your time with other activities like exercise, and started seeing your friends more. Some time has passed, and your resolve is beginning to waiver. Your toxic friend or ex-fiancé have found other ways to contact you and although you haven't responded to these messages, you begin thinking about them all the time. You begin to wonder if you made the right decision in leaving. Each day away without contact seems to feel more and more difficult. And you consider going back to the former relationship. But instead of going back to old, unhealthy behavior, I want you to stop to pause and take inventory of how you're feeling, and to remember all the ways in which this relationship negatively impacted you. And what you've gained in the time and space you've given yourself since your separation.

Most people resist change because they focus on looking back towards what they perceived as loss, instead of looking ahead at what they have and will gain from the changes they have begun to implement. What is it that you're gaining? And is this enough to keep you moving forward? If not, then you need to dig deeper to find your 'why', so that you can continue to resist the temptation to return to unhealthy relationships or coping behaviors. If you're trying to climb that hill of change alone, then I implore you to seek out people that would encourage you along the way towards your goals. And while you're climbing, it helps to appreciate where you are, and take a moment to look around and notice what's happening around you. Sometimes we just need to allow ourselves to get outside of our own thoughts and feelings about a situation or circumstance and appreciate our own strength, gifts, talents, and worth. We need to cling on to the hope that our life will continue to move forward in healthy ways, and hold steadfast to our faith and support systems to empower us to keep moving one foot in front of the other.

Healing is hard. It takes time and intention. It takes faith, and accountability, and honesty. It takes courage to enter a vulnerable space to be honest about the ways in which our unhealthy coping has been hurting us, so that we can clearly see our goals ahead. It takes drive and focus. And it takes a community around us to support us along the way. As much of us as this journey requires, our healing gives back so much more if we can remain committed towards our own health and well-being. And the beautiful thing is that our healing sends ripples out to everyone around us, and even down into our future generations. Isn't that what each of us wants in the end? To not only improve our lives, but the lives of our future generations? It is possible to be the person who breaks the cycle of addiction, domestic abuse, self-harm, unhealthy boundaries, the need to control everything, anxiety, depression, fear … the list goes on. You could be the person who learns how to cope with these things in better, and healthier ways, and teach those ways to your children, nieces, and nephews, or other people in your community. You could become the change agent in someone's life so that an entire generation is restored.

I hope you're encouraged today to keep your eyes on the prize, on your restored mental, emotional, and physical health. I hope you're encouraged to find the courage and strength you need to persevere through the fear of change, or confronting the truth about yourself, your relationships, your unhealthy thoughts, behaviors, and coping. But what I hope for you most is that you feel loved and cared about in the process. You were uniquely made and have so much to offer to others and to future generations. I believe in you.

We're almost to the end. I hope you continue to explore the answers to these questions:

- What is holding you back from making the changes you have been trying to make? If the answer to that question is fear, then what is it that you fear?

- Who in your life do you trust to hold you accountable?

- How do you respond to the feeling of giving up, and going back?

- What is your long-term focus, and motivation to make positive changes in your life?

- Do you believe that change can happen? If so, why do you believe this? If not, then what small change can you decide to make today that will help you believe?

- Who can you tell about your decision to change?

CHAPTER NINE:

Sharing is Caring

"We are not cisterns made for hoarding; we are channels made for sharing." [20]

- BILLY GRAHAM

Have you ever thought about what it takes for a child to learn how to share? True empathy, as opposed to mimicking behavior, is such a hard thing to teach. You might see a child take a toy from another, and so you approach the child to get down to their level. It goes a little something like this: "Now Billy, we need to share our toys with Cindy. Cindy gets a turn, too." Or, "Billy, Cindy was playing with that toy. You need to share with her." But what you're teaching the child is to obey your commands, rather than provide an opportunity for the child to really *see* the pain or discomfort their actions caused the other. They don't get the time or haven't developed the ability yet to observe and reflect on their own behavior and then come to a decision on how to repair that momentarily broken connection. It takes time for the child to understand the pain they inflict on others by experiencing the same pain inflicted on them. This deepening understanding of the pain others feel is called empathy, and it takes years for empathy to fully develop in a child or person's brain.

Our experiences allow us to sit just a little longer with the pain of others when we encounter it. We are able to sit beside another person who is hurting, and develop our capacity for empathy towards others within our community and beyond. As we live out our lives, we begin to truly understand some deep hurts like grief and loss, divorce, trauma, and abuse. And because we were made for community, our hearts are drawn towards those who share similar experiences we've been through. When we come across someone we have something in common with we might share things like our time, energy, monetary resources, food from our kitchens, or even our homes with others who are in need. We express a deep-seated desire to lessen their pain—a pain we ourselves have come to know so well. But in the process of sharing the burden of another person's pain, we need to remember to care for ourselves in a way that prevents harm or burnout.

Think about the people in your life and the ways you interact with them. Are there friends or family members who demand more of your time and attention than others? Do these same people require more compassion and patience? Your interactions with each person in your world comes at a cost, whether you're aware of that cost or not. And learning how to implement healthy boundaries around your friendships, family relationships, work, etc. is essential for maintaining the progress you've made along your own healing journey while still engaging in community in meaningful ways. One of my favorite books as a kid was *The Giving Tree* by Shel Silverstein. It is a children's classic and starts with *'Once there was a tree ... and she loved a little boy'*. (Silverstein 1964). Throughout the story, the boy returns, demanding more and more from the tree. The tree, out of love for the boy, continues to give of herself in her desire to make the boy happy. The boy ages into late adulthood, and the tree is reduced to a short, lonely stump on the ground. The boy, now an elderly man, realizes that all he needs is a place to rest, and the tree offers herself a place for the boy to sit. The end. The tree held nothing back from the boy she loved, but we are not fictional trees written into a story. We're people with finite mental, emotional, and physical stores of energy. We need to refuel and aren't impenetrable. Even those of us with the thickest of skins bruise and are easily pierced. Instead of trees planted in the earth, I'd like to compare each of us to a potted plant. We need to be cared for, and given plenty of sunshine, and water. When the soil is dry, it needs to be hydrated else the plant will eventually wither and die.

So practically speaking, what do boundaries look like? And why should we have boundaries? I'll answer the latter and return to the former. We should have boundaries because we want to thrive in this world, and continue to do whatever work we set out to do for as long as we can, especially when the work involves causes or people we're passionate about. We want to enjoy healthy relationships with those around us and have a healthy work/life balance. If we were to give all we have without refueling, or putting in place healthy boundaries, then we limit the amount of time we can help others or engage in those relationships. What do boundaries look like in real life? Setting boundaries is something that starts with knowing your own limits, convictions, needs, and existing responsibilities. It includes monitoring the time, and energy you give to each area, as well as know how best to replenish the energy you spend. Boundaries also include knowing how to say no, well. The word "no" does not need to proceed a lengthy explanation. No can simply be no. And lastly, you need to recognize when one person, or area of your life is demanding more of you than you have to give. If you are unable to recognize unhealthy relationships or boundaries, then this is something you may want to engage a therapist for.

If we continue to live life burned out, we are putting ourselves in a position that threatens our physical and mental health. Not only that, but we are slowly eating away at the health of our relationships around us. Burnout can look like constant anger, bitterness, and resentment towards a particular situation, environment, or relationship. Burnout can look like dropped priorities or low dependability. Burnout can look like apathy towards close relationships. Burnout can look like depression and anxiety. Burnout can look like addiction to video games, social media, or obsessing over purchases, makeup, time at the gym, or any host of things or activities that allow your mind to avoid accountability in any area of your life. When you've entered a state of burnout in one area, you're likely to be suffering in other areas of your life as well. Burnout affects every aspect, and limits our ability to think clearly or make rational decisions. It decreases our ability to handle or respond to stressful situations. This is why it is so important for you to consider ways to protect yourself from fatigue and burnout while caring for others who walk a similar painful path as your own.

Now that we have a better understanding of burnout and what it can look like, let's discuss boundaries. You determine how much you're willing and able to give to another hurting person. But remember, depending on their circumstances, you may not be able to give them all the help they actually need. This is why it's important to understand your ability to help and have the wisdom to step aside so that your friend or family can get professional help. This is especially important when caring for someone with anxiety, depression, suicidal thoughts or ideation, etc. Sometimes our help can make things worse for them. We do not need to fix every single person who crosses our paths, but what we can do is acknowledge their pain and sit with them in it while they get the professional help they need. My daughter is one, and her ability to understand reasoning is obviously impaired by her age and physical development. But when she falls and gets hurt, she understands my soothing tone and gentle embrace. I can communicate my love and empathy to her in a way that she totally understands. Sometimes she is helped and healed just by having someone loving her without judgement, someone holding a space for her to feel her pain. In the case of my daughter, the space I hold for her is my embrace. She lets me know when she feels better and I allow her to make the decision when to part from me. Sometimes the best thing you could do for your friend or family, *and* yourself, is just be available to hold a non-judgmental space for them that is filled with love, and empathy; a safe place for them to experience their pain. When they are ready to part from that space, they will let you know, and in that time span, you will have built trust and credibility with them so they can be more open to seeking out the professional help they need.

Because of your loving, non-judgmental presence, you are now positioned as a safe space for others in your life who need care and support, too. Even so, there will be those that require more professional support, and not every person who needs it will have access to or want to seek it. Sometimes all your attempts at helping this person do not actually help, and they go away from you still hurting or seeking other kinds of support. This is the point when you have to make a decision to either continue to pursue them or allow them to make their own choices for their own care. You can continue to be a supportive presence in their life, though maybe at a distance. What you want to avoid is getting wrapped up in the chaos they're experiencing to the point that your life begins to become a reflection of the chaos happening in their life. Then you both become the person needing help and support, and neither can provide that to the other while in crisis. You may have heard tragic stories of people drowning when they went into the water trying to save a loved one who was drowning, and both drown instead. You want to make sure you are prepared to stay afloat, unaffected, and armed with the proper knowledge, experience, and strength that will allow you to provide aid to someone who is hurting.

After making it through to the other side of your pain and experience feeling healed and whole, you're going to want to take what you've learned or gained to help others along and support them in their pain and suffering. It's only natural to engage in community in this way. You are not going to be able to avoid people or their pain, especially since your own experiences have increased your compassion towards and awareness of others. As with most things, there are ways to do them safely. Helping others is similar. Here are some things to consider, and ways to help prevent burnout while helping others.

- Examine the relationship and the source of your desire to help—do you feel obligated, guilted, or otherwise coerced into providing your time, energy or resources? If so, there may need to be some open communication about how you're feeling in the relationship, or about the help that's needed.

- Understand your own limitations and set proper expectations. This is an important aspect to consider. If someone is asking for two weeks of your time, and you can only give three days, then communicate this. Do not overcommit yourself to more than what you have to give. That goes for time, energy, and resources. Also, know your limits for helping. If you find yourself in an emergency situation that you are not prepared to handle, please don't hesitate to contact emergency personnel.

- Decide on some boundaries and communicate them to another person who can help hold you accountable. This extra accountability will help maintain your own sense of sanity and balance in life, especially if you're someone that knows in advance that you will have difficulty not over-extending yourself. For example, once I provided aid to a friend and really felt like we should open our home up to this person, but realized doing so might jeopardize the safety of our children. My husband was instrumental in reining me in to discuss the logistics of this line of thinking and add perspective to my desire to help.

- Communicate these boundaries to the person seeking support as the need arises. Assertive communication is key when setting up boundaries that help protect you and the other person. I always explain that healthy boundaries aren't meant to separate or distance, but to keep everyone safe. I use the example of painted lines on the highway. They keep everyone safe and moving through life together in harmony. So do healthy boundaries.

- Follow through with your boundaries. Setting boundaries is one thing, maintaining them is another. Ask for help, if you need it, to help with your follow-through. I promise you will feel so much better, and better able to give your all in a situation when you know you're operating within boundaries you've already established.

- Check-in with yourself regularly to take a look at how you're feeling throughout the journey of helping others, be open to seeking help for yourself for any unexpected triggers or threat to your own mental and emotional health. I share about the importance of clear communication with others, but communicating with yourself is just as important. If you notice signs of burnout, please seek help from friends, family, or therapist. Helping fatigue and burnout isn't uncommon, and you aren't alone. Please ask for help!

- Seek out other support for yourself if needed, or consult a professional if the person you're helping needs more help than you're able to provide [see above: understanding your own limitations]. This is especially important for friends or family who are experiencing depression, anxiety, or are engaging in self-harming behaviors or are in an abusive relationship. They call you for help and when you arrive at the situation, it may be beyond your ability. In this case, it's helpful for you to have some hotline or 'warm line' numbers on hand.

- If you feel your person is experiencing an emergency or is in crisis, do not hesitate to dial 911 (999 or 112 depending on where you are located) to get them the help they need, such as the nearest hospital or emergency room. This is always an option for any time you feel the need for some more assistance. Don't feel silly. If you *think* you might need to contact emergency personnel, then you most likely *should*.

My desire for you is that you're able to enjoy the success and healing you have worked so hard for, *and* live and thrive within a vibrant, active, and supportive community. It is so easy to get wrapped up in how good you feel after helping others or walking alongside those with similar struggles. But you are an important part of that equation and deserve just as much care and attention as you're giving out to others. Taking time to learn more about, and practice healthy boundaries and assertive communication will benefit you and every future relationship you engage in.

Take some time to really think about and reflect on these questions and their answers:

- What areas of your life do you lack self-control in?

- Who in your life do you have a hard time saying no to? Why?

- Do you know how to recognize burnout? What do you feel?

- What are some steps you take to set up boundaries, or engage in self-care while caring for others?

- What are some limitations to your help? Do you feel comfortable communicating your limits?

CHAPTER TEN:

On Being a Therapist

"What we know matters, but who we are matters more. Being rather than knowing requires showing up and letting ourselves be seen. It requires us to dare greatly, to be vulnerable." [22]

- BRENÉ BROWN

You've made it to the end of the book, and if I'm being honest, I'm relieved I made it, too! This process has been an emotional rollercoaster and a logistical marathon. I have spent sometimes days and lost hours of sleep trying to piece together a particular section of this book in my mind. I have fretted over every word in each chapter of this book. I have juggled the demands of my infant and toddler, battled against the vestiges of postpartum depression and anxiety, took on the never-ending piles of laundry, and rode the waves of life to make time to write the words you're reading now. But it has totally been worth the time and effort to reach out to you in a meaningful way, to help you understand that you aren't alone on this journey, and to add some humanity to the therapeutic process. And while I've written all the other chapters in this book with you in mind, I saved this particular chapter for the therapist reading this, the person who wants to be a therapist, or the grad student who will soon become one. If you don't fit any of those categories, it's okay. I'd love for you to keep reading anyway, because we've travelled this far together. It's important for you to know what's important for your therapist, too. So, let's lace up one last time, and finish this marathon we started ten chapters ago, shall we?

As I said, this chapter is just for you, therapist. You have endured years of sacrifice to be right here, right now. No doubt you've skipped out on time with friends and family so you could do research or study for exams (remind me to tell you about the time my mind went *completely blank* during a grad school exam.) You've bounced babies on one knee, and written term papers. You've reached Jedi skill level with managing your calendar and schedule, and you've done so with your future clients in mind. We did not enter this feed to earn bucket loads of money, *amiright*? (Spoiler alert: there are no buckets of money.) You might have found yourself relating to the stories you've read in this book. And it's that brush with your own humanity, accepting yourself and others with all their faults yet also being able to recognize their potential that has you running with abandon towards this field. After all, isn't that what this profession is all about? Coming alongside another to help them see and reach their full potential? In reaching so, they can begin to understand the unique process that brings about their own healing. You endured the sacrifice to get where you are in the professional world because you've seen the depths of your own sorrow, shame, regret, and pain. You've dug down deep to unearth the very worst things about yourself and your life experiences. You've examined every minute detail, turned it over, and examined it some more. You were able to engage in your own spiritual and/or therapeutic journey to process what you've found, and found healing. You realized that if you, with all that junk in your trunk, can resurface from the depths healed and whole, then others can too. You felt motivated by your transformation to want to help others along with theirs. But in doing so, I want to remind you of some things. We talked about them in the last chapter. While you're off saving the world, I need you to be super aware of yourself, and your own boundaries and triggers.

Yes, I know this concept has been reinforced dozens of times throughout the course of your educational career and training. But here's the thing: no one can really prepare you for the first time a client in session triggers some unresolved thing deep inside you that you didn't know was there. Or what it will be like to return to work after the loss of a parent, child, or partner. Or the vulnerability you'll feel after a fresh trauma, any kind of assault, or other violation. Life still happens, even after you've found yourself healed and whole. And you owe it to yourself and to the people you'll be working alongside to be fully aware of the potential for these things to affect you as a human being and a therapist. Although we aren't immune to the tragedies of life, we can be prepared to face them within the context of our own humanity and profession.

We aren't robots. I know I keep reminding you of your humanity. Why? Because I have to. If we don't take the time to check in with ourselves our own pride, ignorance, financial needs, or altruistic pursuits threaten to keep us in a constant state of pouring out. I cannot stress to you enough how dangerous this is to your own mental, emotional, and physical health and the people you work with. This self-awareness goes beyond self-care. It is transformed into community care. When you allow yourself to be held accountable, and poured into, then everyone benefits. The great work you've invested years in can continue peacefully, and with some balance. Lives can continue to be transformed. There's a reason why this process is at the top of our code of ethics. And sometimes that process might require you to step away from the profession for a time in order for you to come back a better therapist.

When I became pregnant for the first time, I was elated. But it soon became apparent that my pregnancy was not going to make it to term, and I had a miscarriage. For reasons I couldn't identify at the time, this experience was very traumatic for me. I was working at a very high demand and stressful place and this miscarriage made me realize my priorities were all wrong. When I returned to work, I submitted a four-week notice of resignation and entered therapy to work through some of these unknown things. Sometime later, I discovered I was pregnant again, and I was fearful of another loss. Because I was already in therapy, I continued to process all my issues with becoming a mother, fears surrounding the pregnancy, and abandonment issues I faced because of the decisions of my own mother. I cannot tell you just how healing this time was for me, as I began working a much lighter load at another place of employment. My caseload slowly crept up and I was able to work while healing. But then my son was born, and postpartum anxiety blind sighted me. Although I knew all the signs and symptoms, it still took time for me to recognize what I was truly experiencing. The weeks and months of sleeplessness and hypervigilance triggered other PTSD symptoms from past traumas, and then I knew I was not fit to return to work. I reached out to my boss and resigned from my position, my dream job, so that I could better care for myself and my son. I entered a trauma-focused modality of treatment, and within a few months, I felt myself coming up and out of my battle with postpartum anxiety. A few more months passed as I consistently used the techniques I learned. I was also surrounded by my faith community, friends, and family. It was with their support that I was ready and able to return to work. As I prepared to reach out to my former employer, I discovered I was pregnant again and decided it best to take time to care for myself during my next pregnancy, and prepare for any postpartum symptoms I may experience. I share this with you so that you really understand that it is not only okay for you to seek therapy for yourself, but it is expected of you.

 I have spent chapters of this book encouraging you to throw off the shame our culture or society would have you feel for reaching out for therapy within the context of the average person. But I want to highlight something about our profession that you may already know or realize from your time in it. I cannot tell you the number of times I've heard colleagues express feeling *shame* for seeking therapy for themselves within our profession. Some would even avoid getting therapy for themselves. So, why are we so willing to advocate for our clients but not for ourselves or our profession? We help our clients process through feelings of guilt and shame, yet hold ourselves to a different standard? You are not above the people you walk alongside with. The best decision you could make for yourself and your clients is to continue monitoring your own emotional and mental health, know your boundaries, and seek supervision or therapy when you need. Seeking out and receiving therapy for yourself does *not* make you a bad therapist. Read that out loud if you didn't catch it the first time. As a grad school professor of mine would say, "Let it simmer." Better yet, put it on a post-it and hang it on your bathroom mirror. In fact, seeking out therapy for yourself when you need it makes you an even *better* therapist than you were. That's right, you heard me. None of us in this profession receive medals of martyrdom for pushing through our mental illness, emotional pain, or trauma. Yet here some of us are, pushing through the pain, pretending it doesn't exist. While we're busy plowing through, we leave a wake of unintentional harm to our clients and their families. We would help our clients see the harm these kinds of thoughts and behaviors create, yet we are unable to see it for ourselves. We need each other to stay accountable for our own care. If doctors make poor patients, so do therapists. But it doesn't have to be that way. You can still be a great therapist while going to see your own. You can still be a great therapist and come home to navigate a complicated relationship or parent rebellious teens. Being a great therapist—and living and experiencing life do not have to be mutually exclusive. We aren't impermeable, but we can be held accountable for our own mental, emotional, and physical health and wellbeing.

How do you hold yourself accountable? Do you have a network of supports who speak truth into your life if they notice your self-care or performance slipping? Are you open to stepping away from your work in order to seek the kind of care or time you need to regroup and heal? If the answer to any of those questions is no, then you already have a good starting point in which to put protections in place for yourself and your clients. Knowing yourself, your triggers, abilities, and limitations are key. I have only come across one person that I had difficulty working with. In that instance, a male colleague and I transferred clients. Mine had a cultural expectation of me because of my gender that did not align well with his therapeutic process, but once he switched to a male therapist, he was able to open up and delve into some areas that needed to be addressed. Meanwhile, the female client that was transferred to me was unable to open up to her previous therapist because of the trauma she experienced. She did not feel safe speaking to a male. In both cases, the male therapist and I sat down to come up with a mutually beneficial plan for these two clients and the transition was seamless. We made decisions that were in the best interest of our clients. But the decisions we make in our clients' best interest do not end at the office. The choices we make concerning our own time, energy, resources, sleep, exercise, nutrition, social commitments, spirituality ... and so many more can play into how prepared our minds and bodies are to care for and work alongside each person that walks through our office door. If you are new to the field, and even if you aren't, please do not hesitate to seek supervision. If you are in private practice alone, I hope you are involved in a peer mentor or peer supervision group that can help hold you accountable, and provide knowledge and experience that would help supplement your own.

Lastly, therapist, you matter. Your work matters, but also your mental, emotional, and physical health are just as important. You do not have to be ashamed or fear working through old or new triggers, maladaptive coping mechanisms, or traumas. Please do not feel pressured to work when it would be best for you to have time off and away. Please listen to your mind and body when you're in session to discover if you've come across a boundary or situation that requires supervision. And don't be afraid to allow your humanity to shine through. You see, those broken vessels I talked about at the beginning of this half of the book are still beautiful. They may even be more beautiful after being mended. That broken pitcher may no longer hold water or juice, but flowers instead, to be admired and appreciated. It still holds a place and purpose. And you can as well, even while seeking therapy for yourself throughout your career. Your humanity only brings a depth of compassion and empathy that will help you to better care for your clients.

If you are reading this and you aren't a therapist, then I want to thank you for making it to the end. You see, it's important that we all be reminded of our worth and our capacity for healing and providing light to the path of someone else's healing journey. Each of us, regardless of our profession, or place in life, has the ability to pour into another hurting person. We each have a responsibility to one another to care for and *do no harm.*

I hope that your journey through this book has been an encouraging one. This book is in no way meant to be a substitute for quality professional counseling. However, I hope it opens up your mind to the possibility of sharing your story with someone who is ready and willing to walk alongside you so that you can break old patterns of thinking or behaving, and live a more peaceful and authentic life. I hope this book has helped you to understand that although we all travelled different roads to where we are today, the experience has shaped and molded us into who we are. We are each worthy of love, compassion, patience, and understanding. Our thoughts and feelings are valid, and our experiences are important to the overall narrative in a culture that might devalue or place a double standard on help-seeking. My hope for you is that you would seek out wholeness for yourself even if it requires facing your fears; that you would share your story with someone that can help you make sense of it for you; and that you would engage in the work it takes to discover your value and potential, so that you can live life offering your best, most healed self to the service and betterment of yourself and humanity.

Life is a journey. We do not travel alone.

ACKNOWLEDGEMENTS

- I am so thankful to God for bringing me along on this journey. He has preserved my heart, and mind throughout it all and has always been there for me, loving me, and encouraging me to keep moving forward. I will forever be thankful for His love, and mercy, and grace each day. I especially felt his peace throughout this process as I wrote and prayed for His guidance and direction with every word. Thank you, Father, for making me just the way I am and for showing me a way to care for and love the world.

- I want to thank my supportive parents for being behind me 100% throughout this entire project. We have worked through so much together, and their willingness to have the hard discussions, with love, is amazing to me. God has done a great work there between us and I'm happy to say that we are able to enjoy fruitful and supportive relationships today. Thank you, mom and dad for all your support!

- My husband has been amazing. It hasn't been easy to raise two very young children. We had two under three when I started this process, and he has been the best teammate. Never once has he complained about my long nights away writing, and he has always given his care, love, support, and grace through the ups and downs of this process. MK4E and GTR

- My children have undoubtedly pushed me to be a more compassionate, and loving person. They have shown great patience for such small people throughout this process and have graciously provided me the space I needed to write. They have never complained or shown their disappointment when I had to leave each work night. They just sent me out the door with their love and support. Thank you both. Mommy loves you both *so* much.

- My mothers-in-law have been so very loving and supportive. Amy, your encouragement after reading the first five chapters really gave me the boost I needed to write the last five. Thank you both for loving our children and giving us much needed breaks throughout this last year so we could rest, and recharge ourselves. Thank you for everything!

- Jan and Dave: I cannot believe that we found one another after over three decades! Your love and support have been invaluable throughout this process and in our lives. Thank you both for living life with us!

- Ellen has shared her wisdom and offered her insight throughout this process. She was one of the first people to believe in this book and in me as an author, and for that I will be forever grateful. Thank you for all your encouragement, excitement, and support throughout this project!

- Our publisher, Kristie, has been strong and confident. She has challenged Ellen and me in ways we needed, and shown her unwavering support. She has such passion for this project and has done everything she can to see it through to the end. Thank you for being AMAZING!

- Our contributing authors have been AH-MA-ZING! Their enthusiasm, and support of our mission to reach those who are still suffering in silence has been equal to none. I have really enjoyed working with each of these talented, and passionate clinicians. They have worked hard to help bring this dream to life!

- Missy – you seriously have been my cheerleader from the start. I told you I would mention you in my acknowledgements. You have truly been my 'book doula'. Every time I thought I couldn't keep going, you sweetly reminded me of God's plan and purpose. Thank you for your countless texts, prayers, and affirmations. Thank you for your friendship.

- Laura – thank you for your enthusiasm. I know you couldn't be a part of this book, but you have been cheering me on from the start, and really encouraged me to include Chapter ten in this book. Thank you for reminding me that we should *never* be ashamed as therapists to seek out therapy for ourselves.

- Rachel – you were the first person I read my introduction to. I wrote that in about half an hour and it has stayed pretty true to that first draft. You were the one that wanted *more* from me and couldn't wait to read every word I wrote. I love your sweet mama's heart, and our random chats. You have been an amazing sounding board for my ideas. Thank you!

- Dorothy – I am so honored by your continued friendship. You always believed in and respected my clinical skills from day one! We've had some amazing consults, and just chats about life. Knowing you has made me a better clinician! You let me know every time we speak just how proud you are of me. I value our friendship and look forward to a collaboration in the future!

- Lastly, I saved the best for last: I want to thank YOU (if you've made it this far.) The person reading this now. You are the one that truly kept me going when I had an obstacle to overcome. I hope you know just how cared about and loved you are. And I hope you have been empowered and encouraged to share your story, too, one day.

REFERENCES:

[1] Nichols, M. H. (2019). Morgan harper nichols. Retrieved from https://morganharpernichols.com/blog/tell-the-story-of-the-mountains-you-climbed?rq=mountain

[2] Tew, R. (2015, September 15). I'm Perfect in My Imperfections. Retrieved from https://livelifehappy.com/life-quotes/im-perfect-in-my-imperfections/

[3] King, M. L. (1960). Good reads. Retrieved from https://www.goodreads.com/quotes/26963-if-you-can-t-fly-then-run-if-you-can-t-run

[4] Keller, H. (1903). Psychology today. Retrieved from https://www.psychologytoday.com/us/blog/here-there-and-everywhere/201102/30-quotes-healing

[5] Hebrews. (2017). In *Holy Bible: New International Version*. Grand Rapids, MI: Zondervan.

[6] Richo, D. (2019). Good reads. Retrieved from https://www.goodreads.com/quotes/tag/healing

[7] Kintsugi: The Centuries-Old Art of Repairing Broken Pottery with Gold. (2017, April 25). Retrieved April 19, 2019, from Kintsugi: The Centuries-old Art Of Repairing Broken Pottery with Gold Chattyfeet- Shovova - https://mymodernmet.com/kintsugi-kintsukuroi/

[8] Martin, C.B. (2019). Good reads. Retrieved from https://www.goodreads.com/quotes/tag/support?page=3

[9] Colette Curtis - https://www.townofparadise.com/index.php/visitors/about-paradise

[10] Winsor, M. (2049, February 8). Paradise residents recall horrifying escape from the camp fire: 'This should never happen again'. *ABC News.* Retrieved from https://abcnews.go.com/US/paradise-residents-recall-horrifying-escape-camp-fire-happen/story?id=59933153

[11] Rogers, F. (2019). Good reads. Retrieved from https://www.goodreads.com/quotes/tag/trauma

[12] Montgomery, L. M. (2019) Book riot. Retrieved from https://bookriot.com/2018/05/18/literary-friendship-quotes/

[13] Oldster, K. J. (2019) Good reads. Retrieved from https://www.goodreads.com/quotes/tag/self-talk

[14] De Rossi, P. (2011). *Unbearable Lightness: A Story of Loss and Gain.* New York, NY: Atria. doi:https://www.amazon.com/Unbearable-Lightness-Story-Loss-Gain/dp/1439177791

[15] Williams, T. T. (2019) Good reads. Retrieved from https://www.goodreads.com/quotes/tag/blinded?page=2

[16] Roosevelt, E. (2019) Good reads. Retrieved from https://www.goodreads.com/quotes/tag/personal-responsibility

[17] LaMorte, W. W. (2018, August 29). *Behavior Change Models* [Scholarly project]. In *The Transtheoretical Model (Stages of Change)*. Retrieved June 06, 2019, from http://sphweb.bumc.bu.edu/otlt/MPH-Modules/SB/BehavioralChangeTheories/BehavioralChangeTheories6.html

[18] Addair, G. W. (2014). Retrieved March 26, 2019, from http://www.georgeaddair.com/

[19] Hale, M. (2019) Good reads. Retrieved from https://www.goodreads.com/quotes/862035-it-s-okay-to-be-scared-being-scared-means-you-re-about

[20] Graham, B. (2019) Good reads. Retrieved from https://www.goodreads.com/quotes/733813-we-are-not-cisterns-made-for-hoarding-we-are-channels

[21] Silverstein, S. (2013). Retrieved June 25, 2019, from http://www.shelsilverstein.com/books/book-title-giving-tree/

[22] Brown, B. (2019) Optimize. Retrieved from https://www.optimize.me/quotes/brene-brown/97045-what-we-know-matters-but-who-we-are-matters-more/

RESOURCE LIST:

(by chapter)

Chapter One: Lost and Found by Jacqueline Rech

Theme(s): Childhood sexual trauma, intimate partner violence, divorce, foster care, postpartum depression and anxiety

- **The National Domestic Violence Hotline**

  1-800-799-7233 (SAFE)

  www.ndvh.org

- **Anti-Sexual Violence Organization**

  RAINN. ORG

- **National Sexual Assault 24/7 Hotline**

  1-800-656-4673 (HOPE)

- **Postpartum Depression and Anxiety**

  https://www.mywishformoms.org/

- **Postpartum Support International**

  https://www.postpartum.net/learn-more/anxiety-during-pregnancy-postpartum/

- **National Center for PTSD**

  https://www.ptsd.va.gov/

Chapter Two: Journeys Converging by Ellen Ulmer

Theme(s): Turner Syndrome, intimate partner violence, grief and loss/ loss of a parent, depression/anxiety

- **Mayo Clinic – Turner Syndrome**

    https://www.mayoclinic.org/diseases-conditions/turner-syndrome/symptoms-causes/syc-20360782

- **National Dating Abuse Helpline**

    1-866-331-9474

    www.loveisrespect.org

- **National Resource Center on Domestic Violence**

    1-800-537-2238

    www.nrcdv.org and www.vawnet.org

- **Our House Grief Support Center**

    https://www.ourhouse-grief.org/grief-pages/death-of-a-parent/adult-death-of-a-parent/

- **Anxiety and Depression Association of America – Additional Online Resources**

    https://adaa.org/living-with-anxiety/ask-and-learn/resources#Mental%20Health%20-%20General

- **Battered Women's Justice Project**

    1-800-903-0111

    www.bwjp.org

Chapter Three: Permission to be a Human by Lauren Falgout

Theme(s): depression, anxiety, self-harm, suicidal ideation/attempts, disordered eating

- **Suicide Hotlines and Text Lines across the US**

    Text CONNECT to 741741

    Call 1-800-273-8255

- **Suicide Prevention and Awareness Websites**

    https://suicidepreventionlifeline.org

    https://afsp.org

- **Eating Disorder Resources:**

    https://www.nationaleatingdisorders.org/

    https://www.eatingdisorderfoundation.org/

- **NAMI: National Association of Mental Illness**

    nami.org

Chapter Four: Broken Together by Michelle Tanner

Theme(s): intimate partner violence, faith and spirituality, codependency/love addiction

- **Futures Without Violence: The National Health Resource Center on Domestic Violence**

    1-888-792-2873

    www.futureswithoutviolence.org

- **National Center on Domestic Violence, Trauma & Mental Health**

  1-312-726-7020 ext. 2011

  www.nationalcenterdvtraumamh.org

- **National Domestic Violence Hotline**

  1-800-799-7233 or TTY 1-800-787-3224

  Secure online chat at http://www.thehotline.org/what-is-live-chat/

- **Co-Dependents Anonymous International**

  http://coda.org/

- **What is Love Addiction? – Psychology Today**

  https://www.psychologytoday.com/us/blog/finding-new-home/201902/what-is-love-addiction

- **Book:** The 5 Love Languages by Gary Chapman

- **Book:** The 5 Languages of Apology by Gary Chapman and Jennifer Thomas

- **Book:** Codependent No More: How to Stop Controlling Others and Start Caring for Yourself by Melody Beattie

Chapter Five: Breaking Stigma by Patrick McElwaine

Theme(s): grief and loss/ loss of a parent, addiction

- **Our House Grief Support Center**

  https://www.ourhouse-grief.org/grief-pages/death-of-a-parent/adult-death-of-a-parent/

- **Substance Abuse and Mental Health Services Administration**

  https://www.samhsa.gov/

- **Al-Anon Family Groups** – organization to support families and spouses of people struggling with alcohol dependence

  https://al-anon.org/

- **Alcoholics Anonymous**

  https://www.aa.org

- **Narcotics Anonymous**

  https://www.na.org

- **Medically-Assisted Recovery Anonymous**

  http://mara-international.org/

- **SMART Recovery**

  https://www.smartrecoverytest.org/local/

- **Book:** Loving an Addict, Loving Yourself: The Top 10 Survival Tips for Loving Someone with an Addiction by Candace Plattor

- **Book:** Addictive Thinking: Understanding Self-Deception by Abraham Twerski

Chapter Six: My Tapestry by Veronica Singleton

Theme(s): parent dealing with addiction, childhood neglect, personal mental illness

- **Al-Anon Family Groups** – organization to support families and spouses of people struggling with alcohol dependence

    https://al-anon.org/

- **Adult Survivors of Child Abuse**

    http://www.ascasupport.org/

- **Rethink Mental Illness**

    https://www.rethink.org/

- **Beyond Blue** – support for anxiety, depression, and suicide prevention

    https://www.beyondblue.org.au/

- **Blog Article: How to Recognize and Overcome Childhood Emotional Neglect**

    https://www.goodtherapy.org/blog/how-to-recognize-overcome-childhood-emotional-neglect-0218165

Chapter Seven: Between Two Worlds by Chun-Shin Taylor

Theme(s): Immigration, divorce

- **The National Immigrant Women's Advocacy Project**

    (202) 274-4457

    http://www.niwap.org/

- **Asian and Pacific Islander Institute on Domestic Violence**

    1-415-954-9988

    www.apiidv.org

- **Divorce Care for Kids**

    https://www.dc4k.org/

- **Mom's Divorce Support**

    http://www.momsdivorce.com/

- **Divorce Care – Faith Based Divorce Support Organization**

    https://www.divorcecare.org/

Chapter Eight: Perfectly Imperfect by Tammy Rovane

Theme(s): Parents with addiction, childhood sexual trauma, infidelity, divorce, personal mental illness

- **Sidran Institute – for people who have experienced traumatic life events**

    https://www.sidran.org/

- **Safe and Sound – Organization to help prevent child abuse**

    https://safeandsound.org/about-us/

- **The Significant Other's Guild to Dissociative Identity Disorder**

    http://www.toddlertime.com/dx/did/did-guild.htm

- **The road less travelled: how to support your dissociative partner, Parts One and Two, by Rob Spring**

    https://information.pods-online.org.uk/the-road-less-travelled-part-one-how-to-support-your-dissociative-partner/

- American Association for Marriage and Family Therapy - Infidelity

    https://www.aamft.org/Consumer_Updates/Infidelity.aspx

- Loving a Trauma Survivor: Understanding Childhood Trauma's Impact On Relationships, Robin Brickel, MA. LMFT

    https://brickelandassociates.com/trauma-survivor-relationship

- Supporting Someone Who Has Been Raped or Sexually Assaulted

    http://www.healthyplace.com/abuse/articles/supporting-someone-who-has-been-raped-or-sexually-assaulted/

Chapter Nine: Bitter or Better by Danielle Proch-Vonbartheld

Theme(s): adult exposed to domestic violence and mental illness at home as a child, grief and loss/ suicide of spouse

- **Break the Cycle**

    http://www.breakthecycle.org/

- **Suicide Awareness Voices of Education (SAVE) – Grief Support for Suicide Loss Survivors**

    https://save.org/what-we-do/grief-support/

- **Suicide Prevention and Awareness Websites**

    https://suicidepreventionlifeline.org

    https://afsp.org

- **Book:** Understanding Adult Survivors of Domestic Violence in Childhood: Strategies for Recovery for Children and Adults by Gill Hague

Chapter Ten: Blessed by the Broken Road by Kesha "The Confidence Converter" Jackson

Theme(s): Mental illness of sibling, bullying, intimate partner abuse

- **INCITE! Women of Color Against Violence**

    www.incite-national.org

- **Women of Color Network**

    1-800-537-2238

    www.wocninc.org

- **The Women's Initiative**

    https://thewomensinitiative.org/groups-social-support

- **Blog:** 15 Mental Health Podcasts for People for Color by Davia Roberts

    https://www.redefineenough.com/blog/15-mental-health-podcasts-for-people-of-color

- **Project LETS – support, education, and advocacy for people with lived experience of mental illness, trauma, disability, and/or neurodivergence**

    https://www.letserasethestigma.com/about

- **Institute on Domestic Violence in the African American Community (IDVAAC)**

    http://idvaac.org/

Chapter Eleven: Grieving with Grit, Grace, and Gratitude by Alyssa Gavulic

Theme(s): grief and loss/ death of a spouse, suicide, homicide

- **The Compassionate Friends – Supporting Family After a Child Dies**

    https://www.compassionatefriends.org/

- **Rainbows – Organization offering support to children as they navigate grief and heal from loss**

    https://rainbows.org/about-us

- **National Alliance for Grieving Children**

    https://childrengrieve.org/resources/about-childhood-grief

- **The Dougy Center – The National Center for Grieving Children and Families**

    https://www.dougy.org/grief-resources/help-for-kids/

- **The Centre for the Grief Journey – Loss of a Spouse**

    https://griefjourney.com/startjourney/for-the-grieving-person/articles-for-the-grieving-person/loss-of-a-spouse/

www.ingramcontent.com/pod-product-compliance
Lightning Source LLC
Chambersburg PA
CBHW021940290426
44108CB00012B/904